FEEDING PLANTS THE ORGANIC WAY

GARDEN MATTERS

FEEDING PLANTS
THE ORGANIC WAY

JIM HAY

WARD LOCK

First published in Great Britain in 1991
by Ward Lock Limited, Villiers House,
41/47 Strand, London WC2N 5JE, England

A Cassell Imprint

Line drawings by Michael Shoebridge

Text filmset in 11/11½ point ITC Garamond Light
by Columns of Reading
Printed and bound in Glasgow
by Collins

British Library Cataloguing in Publication Data

Hay, Jim
Feeding plants the organic way.
1. Gardens. Plants
I. Title II. Series
635.987

ISBN 0–7063–7029–5

CONTENTS

PREFACE

Feeding plants organically is not a new concept. Long before the agrochemical industry was created gardeners grew their plants and vegetables almost entirely organically. Some of the materials they used are no longer acceptable for they are known to be poisonous and dangerous to health. For instance, materials such as red lead, arsenic and caustic soda were commonplace in a Victorian garden. They are poisonous to pests and disease and to ourselves but they did not build up the long term toxic residues we are faced with today when using the agrochemical products, as they were not used in large quantities.

The term 'organic' appeared in the 1940s in the USA when there was a move away from the popular trend to use the newly found chemicals. Why the term was used I am not sure; maybe a more appropriate term would have been 'natural' for in reality this is what we are doing, using natural products coupled with natural laws to create a beautiful garden.

These days the organic techniques have had to become more scientific, especially in the case of food production. Considerable research is being carried out on organic methods which in turn comes down to the amateur gardener, bringing in new ideas and methods.

I started growing organically in the mid 1970s when there were very few commercial products available. Today there are numerous 'organic' products available; there is no need to use chemicals to keep your garden healthy.

J.H.

CHAPTER 1

WHY GROW ORGANICALLY?

Recent concern for the environment has seen 'green' and 'organic' become the 'in' words with politicians, television, newspapers and magazine articles. But what do these words mean to the person in the street?

The 'green' concept is to care for our planet. This is something the Red Indians of America tried to teach us hundreds of years ago but no-one would listen to them. They told us to tread softly on the Earth, as she is our Mother. Instead Western man in particular tramped and stamped, gouged great holes in the earth looking for minerals and fossil fuels, cut down swathes of trees and hedgerows which were holding the soil together with their roots, and thus allowed soil erosion to happen, turning fertile land into deserts. He has also tried to browbeat Nature into submission with chemical sprays of many different kinds instead of cooperating with her and learning to adapt to the lessons she is trying to teach us.

The 'organic' concept is the growing of plants without the use of chemicals, either in the form of fertilizers for feeding the plants or as pesticides or herbicides to kill off pests and weeds. Although the term is mainly applied to food production, organic cultivation does have an important role to play in all aspects of gardening.

Why should we be against the use of these chemical products? Are we not living in an age of new technology and doesn't it make sense to make full use of new inventions and products?

The arguments are long and complex but in simple terms they fall into two categories. The first of these is the damage these products are doing to our environment and the second is the detrimental effect they have on our health.

The chemicals used also fall into two major categories, the fertilizers which have been widely spread on our fields over the past 40 years and the poisons for killing insect life and plants. Organic growers believe both types of chemicals have an undesirable effect on our lives.

CHEMICAL PEST CONTROL

Chemical pesticides are designed to kill and are not selective in what they kill. This means that all the beneficial insects like ladybirds, hoverflies, bees etc, all become victims of these sprays. Life is a chain and everything and everyone is dependent on another. The poisons are absorbed by the plants and insects they contact, many of these are in turn eaten by the animals, birds and fish we feed on. By this means we end up with the residues in our bodies and in many cases our bodies do not know what to do with them. Moreover many of the sprays are not only sprayed directly onto the vegetables which we eat but are also 'systemic', which means they go into the sap of the plant and no amount of washing will ever remove them.

A survey carried out by the Ministry of Agriculture, Farming and Fisheries concludes there is no food produced in this country which does not contain residues of these chemicals.

We also face other aspects of this chemical policy, for aerial spraying is the common method of applying the products. The wind can carry them over a far greater area than that intended and in fact in windy weather spray residues can be detected up to several miles away. Again these residues are absorbed by all living tissue, the plants, animals, insects and of course ourselves.

Our bodies are not made to cope with these products, so they are collected by the organs whose job it is to cleanse our body of toxins, or deposits in our body fat. Our systems are incapable of discharging these toxins and they build up causing us to suffer from allergies and unexplainable illnesses. Some of the chemicals have been shown to be carcinogenic. The disastrous side of all this is that the toxins are passed on to our future generations, the baby picking up its mother's toxins inside the womb and through her breast milk.

All this in the cause of keeping our crops pest free – but have we? Initially the pest has been killed off but so have its natural predators. Mainly due to the sheer numbers of pests around, more of these survive than the predators so the pest has a near unchallenged opportunity to multiply again. This means the sprays are used once more.

Life is not fair, it has given the bad a little more protection than the good and whereas the predator is nearly wiped out, the pest survives to breed immunity to the pesticide. The result? The next spraying session kills off more predators while the pest escapes to breed over and over again and, until a stronger killer spray is used, to become a bigger pest than it was in the first place.

Some pests breed every few days and can develop total immunity to a spray inside a season. As the sprays become stronger the problems of using them multiply.

CHEMICAL HERBICIDES

These are used to kill weeds. Their use is not only found in the agricultural industry, for they are also widely used by councils to weed footpaths, and other areas around trees and fences in parks and playing fields. Herbicides are also used in the amateur garden and allotment.

As with the pesticides they are not really selective, killing off almost anything they contact, including the wild flowers, the hedgerows and even the foliage on the trees. In many cases, users have to wear full protective clothing, even breathing apparatus as the chemicals are so deadly.

Fields of food crops can be sprayed several times during a growing season and even at the end the herbicides are used to kill off the foliage on crops such as potatoes.

Some of these herbicides are known to be very dangerous to health, not only by taking them by mouth as they remain on the foods but they can be absorbed into the body by skin contact.

CHEMICAL FERTILIZERS

Everything in nature lives in harmony with its surroundings. No matter how large or small, everything is there for a purpose and each depends upon the other to keep life in a balance.

Everything which lives upon this planet needs food to sustain it. This food needs to supply everything which the organism cannot produce for itself including vitamins, minerals, protein, carbohydrates and so on.

In an organic garden a plant will get all the nourishment it needs out of the soil by the natural process of recycling waste, with nature releasing the appropriate foods to the plants as and when they are needed. This is done by natural processes which take place in the soil, involving a close relationship between the soil life and the plants.

Chemical fertilizers do not work in this way. They are

artificial products made by scientists to bypass the natural functions of the soil and the plants and to feed the plants only the foods the scientist thinks the plant needs – mostly nitrogen, phosphorous and potassium. These three products are often referred to by their chemical symbols as 'NPK' fertilizers.

The chemicals are made to dissolve easily in the soil water and become immediately available to be taken up by the plant. Large quantities of these fertilizers are used so large quantities are taken up. But as plants like to have a balanced diet, it requires more of other elements not being supplied by the NPK and so it can only absorb these as long as they are present in the soil. As no more will be added by the fertilizer which only contains NPK, the soil will become depleted and the plants become deficient in those missing elements. In the case of our food crops, this results in foods deficient in some elements, which in turn leads to deficiencies in our bodies.

Organic fertilizers, mentioned in later chapters, do not dissolve easily and therefore do not have the same effects on the plants.

A very worrying aspect of the large amounts of NPK fertilizers being spread on the fields is that the rains wash much of it out of the soil and into streams, river, ponds and lakes. Here their presence upsets the natural balance of water, reducing the amount of oxygen available to aquatic life and resulting in these ponds, streams etc becoming unable to support life.

Our drinking water becomes contaminated with nitrates and phosphates which again enter our food chain. Excessive amounts of these are known to have a detrimental effect on our health and there is believed to be a link between nitrates and stomach cancer.

This is a very simplistic explanation, many arguments continue between the agrochemical industry and the environmental groups. However I believe anyone who has read *Silent Spring* by Rachel Carson will need little further convincing that the continual use of chemicals is damaging ourselves and our planet. First published in 1960, the book is still very relevant today.

Although most of the literature on organic gardening is aimed at the agricultural industry and the vegetable grower, organic gardening has a role to play in every garden.

Organic products are safe to use and as many are made from waste products, are obviously much cheaper. However there is nothing in this life for free and the cost is your time. In the end it is worth every minute.

CHAPTER 2

SOIL CONDITION, PLANT NUTRITION AND GROWTH

All living things need food in one form or another to survive and in the case of plants most of the food needed is taken from the soil. As a result, to keep the plants fully supplied with all the nutrients required, new food needs to be added to the soil at regular intervals to replace that being used up by the plants. Without this replenishment the soil will become impoverished and the plants grown in it will become weak and die.

The chemical grower feeds the plants by adding very soluble artificial fertilizers to the soil, whereas the organic grower only uses products produced by natural processes and allows nature to convert these into plant food.

To understand the main differences between these two processes it is necessary to have a brief look at the relationship between the soil, plant nutrition and plant growth.

SOIL CONDITION

Starting with the soil I feel most people can look at different soils and are able to judge which are in good condition and which are not. What is really being looked at is the soil structure. If you pick up a handful of soil and squeeze it, if it is in good condition it will form a ball strong enough to remain in shape but when rubbed between the fingers it will easily break down into particles of soil again. If it is not in good condition it will either fail to hold its shape or become a ball of puttylike material which will not break down easily.

Soil starts off as single grain particles, like grains of sand but very much smaller, and it is the ability of the grains to bind together to form larger particles called 'crumbs' which is of utmost importance in maintaining soil in good condition. It is the crumbs which form the soil structure and produce a good tilth in which to grow. The grains cannot form crumbs on their own but need a 'glue' to bind them together. In technical terms this glue is called a 'colloid'. The most important of these colloids is a material called 'humus'.

Humus can only be obtained by adding organic matter to the soil. In the majority of cases organic matter comes in the form of compost, ie recycled vegetable waste, weeds, grass cuttings etc, or manures or leafmould. To clear up a common misunderstanding humus and compost are not the same thing. We can add a barrowful of compost to the soil but it is not possible to add humus. Humus is produced as a part of the complex chain created when organic matter decomposes into plant food. There will be no humus in the soil unless there is plenty of organic matter, and without humus the soil structure cannot be built up into a healthy condition to maintain good growth.

Looking at the role organic matter plays, we can see that it is turned by the action of soil bacteria, fungi and worms into humus, which in turn becomes plant food. Without organic matter to maintain the right environment, the various forms of soil life are unable to exist.

The rate at which all this activity takes place in the soil depends on the degree to which the soil is disturbed. In woodland areas the decomposition is relatively slow whereas in cultivated farmland and gardens where the soil is continually being turned over, the process is much faster.

If there is no replenishment of the organic matter on these soils, eventually all the natural humus and plant food is lost. If this happens, not only will the growth of the plants be affected but without the humus there will be a breakdown of the soil structure as the particles are no longer held together by the 'glue'. The effects of this are soon evident; the soil packs under heavy rain, or after short periods without rain the soil rapidly dries out and in extreme cases soil erosion occurs.

Humus has other roles to play in the soil. It acts as a sponge retaining moisture and plant nutrients, and it darkens the soil enabling it to warm up quickly in the spring and retain the heat into the autumn.

The importance of humus was summed up by the late Dr. Shewell-Cooper who wrote 'A man without blood is dead – soil without humus is equally dead and useless'. A chemical fertilizer does not add organic matter to make humus, it is purely a powdered material containing the basic elements of plant growth.

PLANT NUTRITION AND GROWTH

To remain healthy a human needs a diet consisting of many nutrients and so do plants. This is particularly important for vegetables, for if they are to supply us with all the goodness we need then the vegetables must contain it themselves. Although a plant can be fed through the leaves by using a foliar feed, the major process of feeding is carried out by the roots. The roots absorb water and the food elements made available to them within the soil. Roots perform the other function of holding a plant in position, so it is important that the plant has a fully developed root system or it will die either by being blown over or from lack of food.

There is a close working relationship between the soil, the plant roots, the organic matter and fertilizers, the bacteria, fungi and worms living in the soil. Organic plant food is not in a form which makes it easily absorbed by the plants. The minute creatures living in the soil are capable of transforming it into the composition needed. The roots in turn provide food for the soil life and so the cycle goes on. Everything is relying upon the other to survive. There is harmony and balance in an organic soil, every nutrient a plant needs is available to it.

Worms also need organic matter to live and in return they digest it into a very rich plant food. Their burrowing aerates the soil, creating drainage channels to maintain the correct amount of air and moisture needed by the plants.

Hence the reason why organic gardeners say they feed the soil to feed the plants.

Chemical fertilizers do not work in this way. They are not a balanced plant food, just NPK. They are very soluble, easily absorbed by the plant regardless of the soil life. They do not add organic matter to encourage the soil life to exist, in fact they are known to suppress its activity and even kill it off.

Plants which are overdosed on nutrients do not grow healthily. Hence we can see all sorts of symptoms appearing. Nitrogen is the most dangerous, and in small overdoses unhealthy, leggy, sappy plants are the result, lacking the strength to resist pest and disease attack. In extreme overdoses the cell structure within the plant is destroyed and the result is wilting and eventually the plant will die.

It is difficult to overdose with an organic product, as in the majority of cases applying too much simply wastes your money.

CHAPTER 3

COMPOST – THE HEART OF THE GARDEN

There is a saying amongst organic gardeners, 'a healthy soil grows healthy plants which show great resistance to attack from pests and disease'. Much of the agrochemical industry has labelled this an 'old wives' tale' but now the scientists have been able to prove that the saying contains a great deal of truth.

Work carried out by Cornell University in the USA has shown that when plants are subjected to stress, such as struggling to survive in poor growing conditions, they produce a natural chemical called 'Gluthathione' which increases their vulnerability to attacks by pests and disease. This chemical also has the effect of giving the pests immunity to pesticides, making it even more difficult to remove them from the garden.

It is therefore important that we keep our soil in the healthiest condition possible. Not only will we be saving ourselves a great deal of trouble and expense by deterring pests and disease but the plants give us their best in return, either by their beauty in the flower garden or food value in the vegetable patch.

Organic gardeners feed the soil to feed the plants so our aim must be, by natural products to replenish the food taken out during the previous growing season and, if possible, more than compensate for the nutrients used so that the soil fertility is built up to its maximum level.

In other words, our aim should be to hand over the soil to our future generations in a better condition than it was given to us.

PRINCIPLES OF COMPOST MAKING

The basis of this process is to add organic matter to the soil, the principle of 'returning to the soil what belongs to the soil'. There is no better way to do this than to make compost from all the garden waste. In fact any material of organic origin from around the house can be made into compost. The obvious materials which should be exluded are the man-made materials such as metals, plastics etc, and unless you become very good at making compost, diseased garden waste should be avoided as well. Hardwood prunings will be dealt with later on but everything else from the garden, all kitchen food waste, daily newspapers, hair trimmings, even feathers from old pillowcases can all in one way or another be broken down to feed the soil.

However there are a few tricks of the trade to be learnt for it is almost as easy to make poor compost as it is to make good, so before rushing out to start a compost system it is important to understand a little of the processes involved in the conversion of your waste. It is very complex so we will only scratch the surface in trying to understand what happens in a compost heap.

The main requirements for making compost are air, heat and moisture. The initial stages are carried out by the oxygen-loving (aerobic) bacteria and fungi, so it is essential to have plenty of oxygen (air) available. Any lack of air at this stage causes putrefaction of the decaying waste, with the unpleasant smells which are so common with poor compost-making systems. Moisture is also needed by these aerobic bacteria and fungi, but too much will prevent good aeration of the heap, which again will encourage putrefaction. Heat is generated in the early days of decomposition and temperatures as high as 82°C (180°F) can be reached. The heat generated encourages the bacteria to multiply and go about the good work of digesting the waste and turning it into compost. This heat-generating action only lasts for a limited period and needs to be rekindled by encouraging more air into the heap. This is similar to the old days of coal fires when a good blow with the bellows would make a dying fire burst into flames again. In the case of the compost heap the action of the bellows is replaced by the act of turning over the semi-rotted waste with the garden fork, fluffing up the pieces to ensure plenty of air is trapped in the layers of the heap as it is rebuilt.

Heat also plays an important role, that of sterilization. To kill off any weed seeds or diseased material, temperatures of 49°–71°C (120°–160°F) are required. This is why badly made compost heaps, which do not build up sufficient heat to sterilize the ingredients, can spread weeds and even disease.

Some of the commonest items out of the garden added to the compost heap are weeds and many complain that their compost only spreads them. Let me assure you it is not the fault of the compost heap, but the maker who has failed to develop the heat necessary to kill off the seeds.

You may feel I have over-elaborated this point of generating heat, but it is the essence of good compost making and I believe it cannot be emphasized too strongly. I make no apology if the point is raised again.

The later stages of the compost process are carried out by the anaerobic bacteria (those which do not require oxygen) and the worms. Heat is not required during this stage, in fact too much heat would discourage the bacteria and the worms from entering the heap.

Many gardeners like to add an activator, usually

simply a source of nitrogen, to encourage the build-up of the bacterial activity and increase the speed at which the decaying waste is broken down.

THE COMPOST PROCESS

Reading any gardening book written in the last 20 years or so, you would see the conventional method of making compost is to set aside an area in order to build a heap from 1.35 m (4 ft) square, up to 3 m (10 ft) long by 1.8 m (6 ft) wide, adding an activator every 15 cm (6 in) later and watering thoroughly if the material becomes dry. This continues until the heap is about 1.35 m (4 ft) high, when it is covered with old sacking or similar to keep the heat in and the rain out.

After three to four weeks the whole heap is turned over to entrain more air into it and keep the heat generation going. You can see that in fact the space required is twice that of the size of the heap, to allow for this turning over to take place.

This system is still in use and I have seen some beautiful compost made in this manner, but for the average small garden it is totally out of the question for it has several disadvantages:

1. To build up the heat and retain the moisture within it, the heap has to be built quickly, preferably within a couple of days. It is difficult to collect and store sufficient waste where there are space restrictions to enable this to be done, even assuming the smallest size of heap.

2. The turning over of the heap after three to four weeks is a mammoth task.

3. It will take six to nine months before this compost is ready to use and there is always a certain amount on

the outside of the heap which has not rotted down sufficiently and needs to be recycled.

What is needed in the small garden is to be able to compost small quantities of waste as and when available, and to have converted it into a condition for putting back on the soil within three months.

WHERE DO WE BEGIN?

When I first became an organic gardener, I was advised to allocate 10% of my growing area to compost making. At that time it appeared to be an excessive amount of space to give up, especially as it would come out of my vegetable plot, but I soon found it repaid itself over and over again.

I also learnt that the waste material became usable compost in a much shorter period of time if the aerobic and anaerobic processes were separated from one another.

To do this, and as we will only be dealing with small amounts of material, we need to look at what equipment we will need. Most of the modern compost techniques use containers of one sort or another.

THE COMPOST BIN

Small amounts of waste will not generate heat by themselves so they need to be enclosed in a container, usually called a 'compost bin'. There are many makes available from garden centres and mail order suppliers, mostly of plastic or glass fibre construction, all professing that they make the best compost. Before deciding on which to buy or build, let us remember the essentials for compost making – air, heat and moisture. Firstly, the bin should not have a bottom as the waste material sits on the soil to allow any excess moisture to drain away before it creates an unpleasant smell. Some of the bins have holes in the side walls, supposedly to allow air into the bin, but I believe these are detrimental to the process for all they do is let the cold in, making it difficult to reach the high temperatures needed to sterilize the contents. The act of turning over the contents at regular intervals will entrain all the air that is needed. A good tight fitting lid is needed to keep out the rain.

The bin should also be constructed so that it is stable and not easily blown over in strong winds.

In the UK, the ideal bin is one produced by Sinclair Horticultural called a 'Garottabin'. It will hold about 0.2 cu m (7 cu ft) of material, which is about the same amount the average garden will produce each week (Fig. 1). It is conical in shape and of lightweight construction, making it very easy to lift and leaving the contents in place on the soil.

These bins do tend to be expensive but they will last many years if handled correctly. A cheaper alternative can be made of a standard plastic dustbin. Buy a good quality bin, for the bottom is cut out and the sides must be capable of supporting themselves. The bin is turned upside down and filled through the cut-out in the bottom. The bin bottom is then used as a lid, so consider this point when cutting it off. Failing that, use the original lid. It will be too large, but can be held in place with a brick. The volume of material a dustbin will handle is much less than the bin especially designed for the job, but you can buy several dustbins for the price of the other.

As the heating cycle is only a short period in the time taken to make compost, the semi-rotted waste can be transferred to another type of bin for the later stages of decomposition to take place. The best bin for this is the 'New Zealand' bin. It is of wooden construction (see

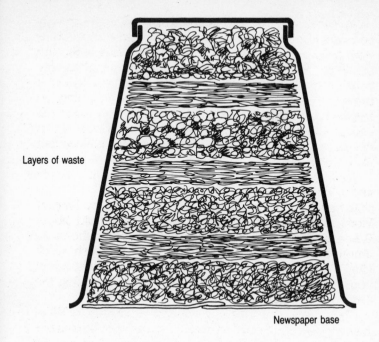

Layers of waste

Newspaper base

FIG. 1 The Garottabin.

page 29) and is a more permanent fixture in the garden, so the next point is to decide where to site the compost area.

SITING THE COMPOST AREA

The site does need to be properly considered. To keep changing your mind can incur a lot of work so it pays to think carefully and make the right decision first time. The area needs to be as level as possible and situated on the soil, not on a concrete or flagged area. This is because we need to drain off excess moisture and in the later stages we need to encourage the worms and other soil life into the bins to play their role in the process.

Access is also very important for not only will you be bringing in waste which may be bulky or in polythene bags, but when the compost is ready a barrow will be needed to transfer the compost to the growing areas. Do not forget where the compost will be needed most for there is little point in having the compost area in an unwanted out-of-the-way place if it involves a great deal of to-ing and fro-ing to spread it. A compromise of all these points may have to be considered.

For the sake of your own household and also the neighbours, the cosmetic side is important. The area can be fenced off and the fence used to support some climbing plants to hide what is happening behind it. However, hiding a heap will not detract from unpleasant smells, and I will say it again – a smelly heap is not making good compost, nor is it maintaining good relations with your neighbours!

COMPOST MAKING

STAGE ONE

The procedure is very simple. Place the bin on the soil in the compost area and gather together sufficient waste material to fill it. Put three or four sheets of newspaper on the soil inside the bin as this makes it easier to collect all the rotted material without picking up too much soil when turning over the heap. Start layering in the waste, dusting each 10–15 cm (4–6 in) layer with two or three handfuls of calcified seaweed. This adds essential trace elements to the compost as well as the calcium content, ensuring the correct pH level is maintained. It is possible, but not essential, to aid the composting process with an organic activator such as 'QR Compost Activator' or 'Fertosan Compost Maker'. These are added in accordance with the manufacturer's instructions.

A large proportion of the composition of vegetables is water – sometimes as much as 90% – and this is released during the rotting process. Examine the waste being added to the bin for if large amounts of vegetables are going in, the contents can become very wet. To avoid this, some absorbent material to soak up the water needs to be added. Grass cuttings are ideal but if not available then newspapers or egg trays are just as effective. Layer the absorbent material every 10–15 cm (4–6 in) and continue until the bin is full.

Do not compress the material and try to push a bit more in, anything left over can be put in a sack and kept until the next filling. Put the lid on the bin and leave it untouched for a week. Do not add any more material to the bin after the initial filling for the bin will have already started to heat up to the high temperatures needed to sterilize the contents. Fresh material is 'cold' and, if added at a later date, will cool off the heat in the bin and weedy or diseased compost can be the result.

As the bin will only be filled once a week the waste material collected should be kept in polythene sacks (old fertilizer bags are ideal) until it is needed. In the middle of summer a number of sacks will be filled and these should be emptied in rotation to ensure putrefaction does not start inside, causing smells and inconvenience to your neighbours. When adding weeds, knock off as much of the soil from the roots as you can before adding to the bin because soil is a cold material and takes a lot of heating up, delaying the heating of the bin contents. The best way of handling weeds is to store them for two to three weeks in a polythene sack so that they have already started to rot down.

At the end of the first week the level in the bins will

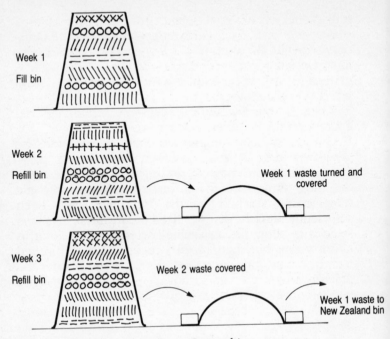

FIG. 2 Making compost using a Garottabin.

have dropped to about half if the process is working properly. The contents of the bin will have started to lose their appearance and there will be signs of water being released. During the winter months, as the weather is much colder, the action in the bins is reduced and the level is slower in dropping.

During the first week (Fig. 2) the bin will have heated up to a temperature of around 71°C (160°F) and started to cool down. A second heating period can be introduced if more air is entrained into the contents. This is done by lifting the bin off and placing it on the soil alongside the contents. Put fresh newspaper in the bottom and then refill it with the now semi-rotted material, loosening it up as it goes back into the bin to trap plenty of air. Replace the lid. No more calcified seaweed or activator is added. Despite the fact the bin is only partially full, do not add more fresh material. This must be left for a second week to ensure the heat is generated and the compost is completely free from weed seeds and disease.

When the bin is removed after the second week the contents will be even less in volume and will be beginning to look like compost. No more heat will be generated even if the contents are turned over again. The first stage in compost making is finished and it is the most important, for if carried out correctly the temperature reached in the bin will have been sufficiently high to have sterilized the material. The next stage is to allow the anaerobic bacteria and the worms to carry out their part in the process. The semi-rotted material now only requires to be kept warm and protected from the rain and this is easily done by either covering it where it lies with 500 gauge black polythene sheeting or by putting in into a New Zealand bin (Fig. 3).

You will have worked out by now that it has taken two weeks to produce a handful of compost and if sufficient amounts are to be made to make an impression on the soil fertility, then a means of increasing the turnover must be found. As an empty bin must always be available to put the fresh material in at the end of the first week, the contents can be turned over on the soil and covered with polythene to release the bin for the fresh material. At the end of the second week they are put into the New Zealand bin as before. This means you will have to allow space for the compost bin and at least one pile of compost under polythene. Another way is to have two bins, a bit more expensive than the polythene sheets but more tidy to look at and less likely to blow about in the wind.

By this method, waste material is converted into good

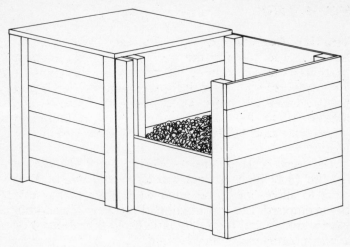

FIG. 3 A New Zealand bin.

sterile compost within 10 to 12 weeks during the summer months. The cold weather will slow down the process so waste laid down in mid to late autumn will not be ready until the following spring.

One point I should make clear is that it is almost impossible to make sufficient compost to meet all your needs. The more land you have, the more compost will be needed involving enormous quantities of waste and time to collect it.

Another point to note is that manures are not used in this method of composting. Manures can either be added directly into the New Zealand bin or better stacked at one side and covered with black polythene sheeting to keep warm and give protection from the weather.

STAGE TWO

The New Zealand Bin   I have already mentioned the
New Zealand bin for the second stage of compost
making. I like this type of bin as it keeps the compost
area neat and tidy, using the space more efficiently and
being aesthetically more acceptable than a heap. Heaps
tend to sprawl over the ground as they are built up and
black polythene is not the most attractive product to
look at.

The New Zealand bins measuring 1 m (3 ft) square
by 1 m (3 ft) high are not too large and are built in
pairs to allow one to be filled while the other one is
being emptied. The construction of the New Zealand bin
is very simple and costs very little if old floor boards or
other secondhand timber is used.

Start off by marking out the bin area 1 m (3 ft) wide
by 2 m (6 ft) long and also the mid points along the 2 m
(6 ft) length. This in effect marks out two adjacent areas
1 m (3 ft) square. Now drive six posts into the ground at
the corners of the area and the marked mid points. The
posts can be 5 cm (2 in) square or 8 cm (3 in) square
and need to be at least 1.5 m (5 ft) long to leave 1 m
(3 ft) of post above the ground. In soft ground it is
worthwhile concreting the posts in position, otherwise
they may move with time.

Next fill in the back of the bin with 15 cm (6 in) wide
by 2.5 cm (1 in) thick by 2 m (6 ft) long boards butting
each to the other so that there are *no* gaps between.
Repeat with the two ends and the centre section to form
two three-sided bins.

Using 5 cm by 2.5 cm (2 in by 1 in) section timber 1 m
(3 ft) long, attach to the sides and centre section
adjacent to the front posts to form a groove wide
enough to allow the front boards to slide up and down.
The front boards are not fixed to the posts for they need
to be removable. It is easy to fill a bin with fixed sides

29

but very difficult to empty it.

Some form of covering is needed for the top to keep the rain out and the warmth in. This again can be of wood, either in one piece to cover both bins or split to have a lid for each.

It is best if the wood is given a coat of preservative before assembly, using a garden-friendly preservative such as the green or clear Cuprinol. Creosote is not recommended as the fumes are not conducive to good bacterial activity within the compost.

For those who are not of a DIY nature it is possible to buy a purpose-made box ready to be assembled in the garden. It is called the 'Organibox'.

The New Zealand bin can be adapted to do the complete composting process without the need to use a plastic bin. A three-bay bin is made by splitting one of the bins into two. The process is then: week one, bay 1 is filled; week two, this is turned into bay 2 and bay 1 refilled with fresh material; week three, bay 2 is turned into bay 3, bay 1 into bay 2 and bay 1 is filled with fresh again. This is repeated until bay 3 is full, when it is either left or removed and stacked on the ground, and covered with black polythene.

I can make about two to two and a half tons of compost a year through my two Garottabins and a pair of New Zealand bins. It may sound a lot of compost but, as users of this material will be aware, it is very little when maintaining a highly fertile garden.

Compost tumbler Another tool available on the market is the 'Compost tumbler'. This is a recycled 220 l (50 gal) plastic drum with a screw-on lid, mounted about its centre on an aluminium frame so that it can be rotated by gripping the base and turning it upside down. The waste is put in the barrel and it is rotated every day and after about two weeks it is removed to a New Zealand bin or stacked and covered as before.

There is the disadvantage that if filled too full once the material begins to break down and release its water content, the bin becomes very difficult to turn over as all the weight is concentrated in the bottom. Although holes in the bottom allow a certain amount of water to escape, turning over does become a strenuous task and not a job for the weak or elderly (I have seen the aluminium frame split with the effort needed to turn an overfilled drum).

It does, however, generate heat inside and makes good compost; but if a sizeable quantity is needed then more than one tumbler is required, for unlike the other bin methods the material stays in the tumbler for the two weeks.

CHAPTER 4

FEEDING THE SOIL WITH COMPOST

Having made all this beautiful compost what do we do with it? As I have said before, it is the major source of organic matter added to the soil by the amateur gardener. There are popular methods of doing this.

DIGGING

Most gardening books recommend that the soil is dug over some time between autumn and spring. This gives the opportunity to aerate the soil, particularly in the vegetable patch where it may have been compacted by constant walking, let the frost break up sods of heavy soils and of course add the compost.

When digging there are a few basic rules to follow. The most important is to go steadily and avoid rushing into the task and doing too much at any one time. Those without experience in this activity will only find it means 'aches and pains' the next day if too much is done at once. Mark out the area to be dug into small sections and concentrate on these one at a time. Use the right tool for the job – a spade is the best in most cases but on heavy soil a fork is more useful and much easier to use. Whichever is used it should be pushed vertically into the soil, not at an angle, and pushed in until the foot touches the ground. Keep the tools clean – there is no point in moving the same piece of earth several times simply because it is stuck on to the spade or fork. When adding the compost, mix it well with the soil in the trench as it is being filled in.

THE 'NO-DIG' METHOD

Despite the fact many gardeners enjoy digging – and I feel in many cases they do it more for their own pleasure than for the benefit of the soil – there are several disadvantages.

1. It is not always possible to dig in the flower and herbaecous borders if they are full of plants.
2. Digging is hard work and some people are not capable of doing large areas.
3. Digging disturbs dormant weed seeds, which helps to create a fresh crop of weeds the next season.
4. Why mix the compost into a spade depth of soil when the plants prefer it in the top 5–10 cm (2–4 in)?
5. The bacteria live in layers in the soil and, if disturbed by the spade, will not be active in breaking down the compost until they have made their way back to their respective layers.

As a result many organic gardeners believe the only way to add organic matter to the soil is by the 'No-Dig' method and the most popular approach to this is by mulching.

MULCHING

Mulching is purely the act of laying the organic material on top of the soil surface. It has the advantage that it can be carried out at all times of the year, except when the weather is frosty. This is because if the frost is buried it will remain frozen for a long time, keeping the ground cold and delaying the start of sowing and planting out in the spring. In actual fact the mulching technique is so flexible that during the summer months uncomposted grass cuttings and shreddings can be laid straight on top of the soil.

Mulching not only is one of the best ways to feed the soil, it is also the best at retaining moisture. Applications laid down after a rainy period will keep the moisture in the soil by protecting the surface from the drying effect of the sun and the wind. This is especially important during long dry summers.

Although mulching can be carried out at any time of the year the early autumn is the time when it will be most effective in raising the soil fertility. It is also a labour-saving device at that time of the year for it is when the average garden is being emptied of summer grown plants and vegetables, leaving the soil vacant over the winter.

Nature does not like to see bare soil and except under the shade of a tree, bush or hedge she will quickly cover it with a carpet of weeds. We can therefore make use of the mulching technique to control the weed population.

When laying down the mulch, it is also a good time to add the slow-acting organic fertilizers for they will have six months or so to release their nutrients in readiness for the early spring growth.

As it is essential that the soil is moist before being covered, wait until the ground has been thoroughly wetted by the rain if the proceeding period has been dry.

The procedure for this mulching programme is very simple. Apply a dressing of an organic fertilizer, i.e. one of the seaweed products. Do not rake or hoe it into the

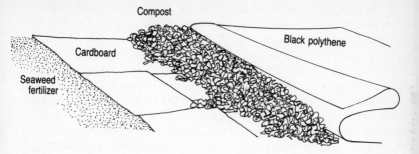

FIG. 4 Feeding the soil by mulching, using cardboard to suppress the weeds.

soil. Cover it with five or six sheets of opened-out newspaper. If the weeds are of the persistent type (horsetail, couch grass, thistles etc,), then spread out opened-out cardboard boxes in place of the newspaper (Fig. 4). However avoid coloured, glossy paper or the waxed type of cardboard. If the weather is windy, spray these with water to prevent them from blowing away. On top of the cardboard/newspaper place an 8–10 cm (3–4 in) thick layer of compost; then if the area is large enough, say more than 2 m (6 ft) square, cover with a sheet of black 500-gauge thick polythene.

The principles behind this are that the fertilizer replenishes the nutrients taken out by previously grown plants, especially the trace elements; the newspapers/cardboard will keep the light away from the weeds and suppress their growth; the compost adds the organic matter to the soil and builds up the humus content, the soil structure and maintains a high level of soil fertility. In addition, the polythene acts as a back-up weed suppressor in case the persistent weeds grow through the newspaper/cardboard as they rot; and it protects the soil from the weather, keeping it warm and preventing the nutrients being washed out by the winter rains.

This technique is ideal in the vegetable garden for the covered area will be in a condition fit for early sowings when the uncovered areas are still wet and cold.

The moisture and warmth retained under the polythene sheeting creates ideal conditions for the worms and soil bacteria to break down the newspaper/cardboard and the mulch, taking them into the top layers of the soil and producing a beautiful weed-free tilth in the spring.

However, if the soil is too dry before the mulch is laid down, these conditions will not be achieved and when the polythene sheet is lifted in the spring the cardboard/newspaper will not have been broken down, nor the compost have been pulled into the top soil by the worms.

As the weeds are suppressed by this method, there is no need for any weeding to be done before laying down the mulch – just cover the ground and forget about them. If however they have grown tall it is better to cut them down and remove them to the compost bins. The roots can just be left in the ground and covered by the mulch.

Leave the black polythene in place until the ground is needed for growing in. There are some gardeners who believe in growing through the polythene by cutting a hole in it to allow a plant to be put in the soil. This is not a good idea for the polythene does not let the summer rain or fresh air into the soil and the conditions underneath the polythene become sweaty and stale. These unhealthy conditions attract slugs which then eat the young plants. Always lift the polythene before planting out.

If early crops are wanted and the weather is still cold, lift only enough of the polythene to allow a cloche to be erected, leaving the rest of the polythene in place.

When the polythene is lifted there is no need to work the soil. Do not remove the mulch (unless the conditions have been too dry and the newspaper and mulch have not been broken down) or hoe, simply smooth the surface with a rake if sowing seed and draw out the drills or dig a hole with a trowel when planting out. The ground will be in perfect condition for growing.

Now I come to the only disadvantage of this method, which is that the polythene has a tendency to blow about in the wind. It needs to be firmly held down at the edges and, if using very large sheets of polythene as I do on my vegetable plot of 4 m by 10 m (13 ft by 33 ft), they need to be held down over the whole area. The edges can be dug into the soil; bricks or bags filled with sand or soil can also be used – anything to keep the sheet in place over the winter months. It will look a bit unsightly but think of the good it is doing to your soil.

CHAPTER 5

WORM COMPOST

I have said anything which will rot down can go through the compost heap, but there is one material which is not recommended for such treatment, and that is food waste. Putting food into a compost bin can attract vermin and even domestic animals to take an interest in the contents, so the best place to dispose of the food waste is in a 'worm bin'.

Worms are an essential element in our soils. In fact it is only where worms are present that soils can be cultivated to give maximum productivity.

There are many different species of worms, but the two we are familiar with are the large earthworm found when working the soil and the small red manure worm so common in compost heaps and manure stacks. It is the manure worms which we can use to our advantage in disposing of our food waste.

Called a 'brandling' by the fishing fraternity, this worm's function in life is to eat dead and decaying material and turn it into a highly fertile soil food, rich in nitrogen, phosphorous, potassium, calcium and organic matter. The worm excretes its own weight of this valuable product every 24 hours so you can see we need a great number of worms to make sufficient quantities of casts for our needs.

Normally, the worms excreta is lost to us in the compost or manure heaps, so the first thing needed is a 'home' in which to provide the ideal conditions for them to live and breed. The worms need warmth (but not heat), moisture (but not too much), plenty of food and a little protein to assist with breeding.

CONSTRUCTION OF A BIN

An ideal home can be made for the worms out of a specially converted dustbin. A standard plastic dustbin with a good tight fitting lid that will keep out unwanted visitors is all that is needed. In order to retain the moisture yet allow any excess water produced from vegetable waste to run away, a sump is made in the bottom of the bin. This is made of a 15 cm (6 in) layer of sand and stones. Builders' 1.8 cm (¾ in) stone is best but anything similar is suitable. Holes are drilled in the sides of the bin at about 5 and 10 cm (2 and 4 in) from the bottom (Fig. 5). The bin is then filled with water until it runs out of the holes. This not only washes the sand between the stones but also moistens it ready for filling the bin.

A piece of wood is then placed on the top of the sump preferably the same diameter as the inside of the bin. This separates the working area from the sump and makes life easier when the bin is ready to be emptied. Plywood and hardboard should be avoided for they will deteriorate with the moisture in the bin. A series of holes need to be drilled in the lid to ventilate the bin, otherwise the worms will suffocate.

FILLING THE BIN

This is not a compost-making process, as there is no bacterial action or heat generation, just the worms eating the waste. As no heat is generated there is no sterilization taking place to destroy any seeds or

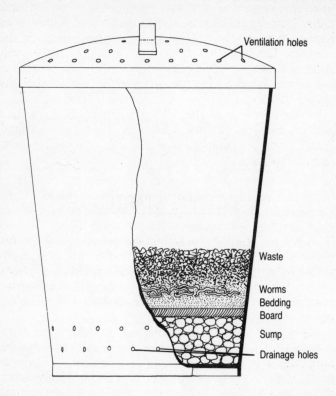

FIG. 5 A worm bin.

diseased materials so it is important that only sterile material is used. The only place we can guarantee not to find weed seeds or disease is in the kitchen so a worm bin is only used for recycling kitchen waste.

Having said that, it is surprising how many seeds are found in a kitchen and as the worm bins provide ideal conditions for germination, quite a number do. It is not uncommon to see tomato, orange, date, melon and many other seedlings growing in the bin. If this does happen it is easy to pull these out and put them in the compost heap. Worms do not eat living material, only dead and decaying vegetation, therefore any seedlings left in the bin will not be touched by the worms but simply left to grow.

All food waste can be added, including meat scraps and bones. The worms will soon clean off any meat, bread, cheese, vegetable waste, and really anything else in the food line.

GETTING STARTED

Now we are ready to start and after constructing the bin the next items needed are the worms. The simplest way is to buy a tubful of worms (brandlings) from a fishing supplies shop. Alternatively, a spadeful of well rotted compost or manure containing plenty of worms can be used.

Place a 2.5 cm (1 in) layer of peat, or the peat substitute coir, in the bottom of the bin. Add the worms and then a little food. Do not overfeed the worms to begin with, a 15 cm (6 in) layer is enough until you see the worms begin to work through this layer, then more can be added. Every time new material is added, fork over the contents. This helps to move the worms into the new waste and keeps the process working speedily. Every 8–10 cm (3–4 in) cover the waste with more peat, coir, even shredded newspaper, which absorbs any moisture released from the vegetable waste and prevents a mould growing on the food waste.

A handful of calcified seaweed added at the same time will help to maintain a neutral pH condition. If the bin becomes too acid the worm activity slows down and the bin will start to smell. Acid conditions are caused by allowing the waste to become too wet or by adding too much of the acid-forming waste such as banana skins, orange and lemon peel.

As the worms digest the food the level in the bin will drop and you may feel the bin will never be filled, but eventually it will.

EMPTYING

It will take six to eight weeks to produce sufficient digested material to make emptying the bin worthwhile. You will be able to judge when the time is right by examining the contents when forking over. Once about half the contents of the bin looks like soil the bin is ready for emptying. Two containers are needed, a wheelbarrow and a polythene sack are ideal. Fork out the contents of the bin into a 1 cm (½ in) mesh riddle and shake over the barrow. The digested material which is dark and peat-like will go through the riddle, leaving the coarse undigested material in the riddle. This is put into the sack along with as many worms as you can retrieve. Some people are a little squeamish about handling worms but I can assure you they do not bite. You now have your starter for the next bin load.

Continue in this way until there is about 5 cm (2 in) of material left in the bin. As this will no doubt contain a number of worms and their eggs this is left, again to help in the building up of the next worm population.

Now empty the coarse reject material and the worms back into the bin and start filling it again with fresh material.

The 'worm compost' is removed from the barrow and kept dry until needed.

If you have room and enough food for two worm bins then the emptying procedure is as before, except that after three to four weeks stop filling one bin while the second is filled. Leave the first bin for a further three to four weeks, turning it over every week, after which there will be a full bin of worm compost. Empty, again riddling the contents and collecting the coarse material and worms to start the next load. This is repeated with the second bin and so on.

USES FOR WORM COMPOST

As it stands, this compost is too rich to be used for a seed potting or growing medium and it needs to be diluted before coming into contact with any roots. As a consequence it is an ideal product if making your own potting composts. A good mix to start off with is:

1 part worm compost
2 parts compost (from New Zealand bin)
1 part peat or coir
all parts by volume.
Add 255 gm (8 oz) calcified seaweed for 9 l (2 gal) bucketful of mixture.

Undiluted worm compost can be used as a mulch material. It will automatically be diluted as it is taken into the soil by the worms.

An excellent tomato feed is a mulch of chopped up comfrey leaves with a 2.5 cm (1 in) layer of worm compost on top. Applied when the first trusses begin to set, this will give the plants the strength to bear a bumper crop of fine fruits throughout the season.

As worm compost is made in a confined area with no need for the bin to sit on the soil or be turned over, it becomes a source of plant food for those who have only a very small garden or even no garden at all. The bin can be placed outside a back door to provide a growing medium for pot plants and for those who wish to grow mustard and cress on the windowsill.

A good mix is one part of worm compost diluted with three parts of peat or coir. Calcified seaweed can be added at a rate of half a handful to a 15 cm (6 in) diameter pot of compost mix.

It can also be used undiluted for pot plants by sprinkling a handful on top of the current soil in the pot. As the plant is watered the goodness in the worm compost will find its way down to the plant roots.

A potting compost made by worms is marketed under the brand name Turning Worms.

CHAPTER 6

SHREDDERS

I have previously stated you will find it difficult to make sufficient compost to meet all your needs. One of the reasons is a shortage of waste to compost, yet there is quite a lot of material around the garden in the form of hardwood prunings and other bulky items which tend to be burnt or taken to the tip because it is difficult to turn them into compost. Such a waste! Some may say that wood ash is good for the garden. They are right, but the return from a bonfire is low in proportion to the amount of material consumed and bonfires are not only antisocial but the smoke is carcinogenic and a hazard to health.

This is where a shredder comes into its own as a valuable tool to have in the garden.

Shredders come in two types, electric motors or petrol-driven engines (Fig. 6). The electric models are aimed more at the amateur gardener, not to say those in this category may not have the need for the more powerful, larger capacity petrol-powered models. However cost will no doubt dictate which version is bought. The electric models come in three sizes and are rated in the electrical unit of energy, the 'watt'. Starting at a 1000 watt-powered motor there are 1300 watt and 1600 watt models; the more powerful models are correspondingly more expensive. Petrol-driven engines are up to 5 h.p. and then the prices rise dramatically.

As with all items you get what you pay for with regard

FIG. 6 A shredder.

to performance. It may be a good idea to get together with other gardeners to share the cost of a unit and then buy the best you can afford. An ideal situation on an allotment.

One big disadvantage with the small electric models is that any large pieces which have to be shredded will have to be cut into smaller pieces before they will fit through the inlet slot. (The slot is restricted in size to stop anyone putting their hands into the shredder.) Further cutting is not always as easy as it may sound. The large models will take whole cabbages and Brussels sprout stalks.

Another point to consider before buying is the machine's noise level. The electric motor is relatively quieter than the petrol engine and you should perhaps bear this in mind if the intended place of use is a residential garden. Why should a petrol-driven shredder be any noisier than a petrol-driven lawnmower? Under the load of shredding the materials the noise increases considerably and will be a nuisance if carried on for any length of time.

In some gardens there is no electricity supply and in this case there is no other option but to choose a petrol-driven model.

SAFETY

Before looking at how to use a shredder one important aspect to consider is *safety*. A shredder can be a very dangerous tool in careless hands. It consists of a set of steel cutters rotating at high speed so there are a number of rules to be followed.

Most importantly, eye protection must be worn as pieces of chipped material can be thrown back out of the feed slot at great speed and with considerable force. Goggles are far better than spectacles as they offer additional protection around the side of the eyes.

With certain types of material the outlet slot can become blocked. To clear this the top cover has to be removed which exposes the cutter blades. *Before the cover is removed the machine must be switched off.* An electric model should be disconnected from the mains to guard against accidently touching the 'on' button. Remember the cutters are designed to chop up materials much more difficult to cut than your fingers!

With electric models always use a 'power breaker' adapter which will provide protection from the risk of electrocution should the extension cable be severed while the machine is switched on, or if the cable insulation or connection gets damp while the machine is in use.

A pair of gloves is advisable as the action of the cutters can snatch material to be shredded out of your hands. Not pleasant if it happens to be rose prunings!

OPERATION

The shredder will cope with almost anything fed to it although it is not too happy with soft, wet material such as vegetable leaves, carrots, tomatoes and the like. These tend not to be formed into chips but more of a pulp. The outlet slot is long and narrow in order to stop inquisitive fingers getting into the cutter blades and as this pulp will not flow along the slot it can cause blockages – a nuisance if the top cover has to be removed every few minutes.

The shredder is designed to deal with the tougher garden materials and in particular the hardwood prunings which no-one would normally consider putting into the compost heap. It is surprising how much of this type of material can be converted into a form suitable for composting simply by shredding.

Shredded material composts very much faster than in the raw state so not only should we consider the tree shrub and rose prunings but also the 'softer' items which still show a reluctance to rot down rapidly. Items such as the potato, pea and bean haulms, bedding plants which go a little 'woody' at the end of the season, herbaceous plants etc. There is no real limit to size for most shredders have a facility to handle up to 1.5–3 cm

(¾–1½ in) thick material. Even newspapers can be shredded. These help to absorb the excessive moisture released from vegetable waste during the composting cycle. All can be converted with relative ease once shredded.

If 'wet' material is to be shredded, then if added gradually with the harder wood (the ratio found mainly by trial and error), a balance between the 'wet' and 'hard' shreddings can be maintained to reduce the incidence of blocking at the outlet.

Care is needed when adding weeds. All too often weeds which have been recently lifted still have a lot of soil on the roots. This soil, especially if it hides stones, can do considerable damage to the cutter blades. Shake off as much soil as possible and check for stones before feeding to the shredder. Preferably let the weeds sit for a day or two to dry out, as by then the roots will be much easier to clean.

HOW TO USE SHREDDINGS

Shredded material can be added directly to the compost bins along with all your other waste. However, just as when handling large quantities of other materials, such as grass cuttings, avoid having a large volume of only one material. The compost process works better and quicker when there is a good balanced mix. This means shreddings should be added a 2.5–5 cm (1–2 in) layer at a time at intervals throughout the filling of the bin. Keep a 5–8 cm (2–3 in) layer for the top. This makes an insulating blanket for the material, helping to generate the heat more quickly and to keep it warm for a longer period.

Shreddings can also be put straight onto the soil as a mulch, as described on page 33. I have seen the most beautiful crop of tomatoes grown in a greenhouse where the gardener placed all the credit on the fact he gave them a thick mulch of shredded Brussels sprout stalks once they were planted out in the greenhouse border. Shredded material used as a mulch can benefit all types of plants, but especially those which are perennial. Plants which come up year after year do tend to be neglected as regards being well fed so a good mulch is a real tonic for them.

CHAPTER 7

COMFREY

Comfrey is a very versatile plant. Some people will regard it as a weed with a very deep tap-root making it difficult to get rid of as any root left in the ground will send up new shoots. Others will regard it as a wonderful medicinal herb called 'knitbone', respected for its ability to help heal broken bones and ease sprains. It is prescribed by herbalists for many other ailments too, either in tablet or cream form. It is also popular as a herbal tea, said to ease arthritis. The organic agriculturalist holds it in very high esteem for its value as a plant and animal feed. It is this latter use of the plant which gave comfrey wide publicity in the mid-1980s, when it was linked as a possible cause of cancer in the liver of animals. Of course everyone panicked, comfrey was put on the list of poisonous plants and the recommendation not to drink comfrey tea was to be read or heard everywhere in the media.

The late Lawrence Hills, founder of the Henry Doubleday Association (HDRA) was a world authority on the plant and had sufficient evidence to show that for comfrey to harm humans it was necessary to drink five cups of comfrey tea every day for 56 consecutive years, in order for the alkaloid assumed to be the cause of the problem to reach toxic levels. HDRA also paid for post-mortems to be done on animals which had died after a lifetime on a comfrey-rich diet. They were all found to have healthy livers.

To deviate slightly, why does the largest organic body in the world have a name 'Henry Doubleday Research Association'? Lawrence Hills in his early days in the organic world studied comfrey closely for its value as an animal feed. It was in the days when everything was rationed just after the Second World War. Lawrence became aware that many animals throughout the world were being kept fit and well with comfrey as a nutritious supplement to their feed. Comfrey, as we know it today, was introduced by Henry Doubleday (1813–1902) who had a contract with the stamp printing company De La Rue to make glue for the stamps. He was looking for a substitute for Gum Arabic (the glue on the back of stamps) and believed comfrey could be a viable alternative. He was wrong, his business was sold and Henry spent the rest of his life studying the plant. Unfortunately, following his death his family, who had considered him a crank, destroyed all his research papers. Lawrence Hills named his association in honour of this forgotten man.

THE COMFREY BED

As comfrey is difficult to eliminate from the garden careful thought is needed in choosing the site before any plants are grown. You could have to live with a wrong decision so, if in doubt, delay; this could be a case of 'he who hesitates is a winner'! Comfrey plants can live for as long as 40 years.

Comfrey will grow in almost any soil and under almost any conditions, even in very shady corners. However we are to use the comfrey as a plant food and if it is to give us the benefit of all the goodness it is capable of absorbing from the soil, then obviously we must offer it the best conditions we can provide to produce good healthy growth. It is the leaves and stems we will be using in our fertility programmes.

Ideally, the site needs to be in the open and not an area where persistent perennial weeds are prevalent or likely to be invaded by tree or hedge roots. Comfrey does not like competing with other plants for the nutrients and moisture in the soil.

The bed should be well dug in the autumn with a generous supply of compost or well rotted manure added and mixed in the top layers of the soil. During digging, remove any weed roots to keep the bed as clean as possible.

Before planting out, dress the bed in early spring with seaweed meal at a rate of 110 gm per sq m (4 oz per sq yd)

PLANTING OUT

Although some seed merchants advertise comfrey seed, it is not advisable to introduce it to your garden because, if it is a seeding variety, any plants left to flower and set seed will result in the plant spreading rapidly through the garden to become a persistent weed. Horticultural comfrey is a sterile variety, and is mostly a hybrid of the common herbalist comfrey and the prickly Russian comfrey. This hybrid known as 'Russian' comfrey is the one introduced into Britain by Henry Doubleday. It is very hardy, surviving the severest of winters. I know of plants which survive year after year in the frozen winters of North America.

Plants can be purchased from the herb section in a garden centre, but they can be expensive bought this way, so a cheaper method is to obtain pieces of root with a growing tip from one of the suppliers selling 'offsets' as the pieces of root are called.

It is even cheaper to get your 'offsets' from a colleague's plants. This is a very simple process. Select strongly-growing plants and push a sharp-edged spade horizontally through the root, about 8 cm (3 in) below the soil surface. This will remove the crown of the plant which will split easily into several offsets. As comfrey is one of the most rapidly-growing plants, the severed root will soon show new growth and be as good as ever within a few weeks.

Only do this when you are ready to plant out the offsets. Do not 'heel' them in until later as they will take root and may end up as another comfrey bed if left in position for too long.

Plant out with 60 cm (2 ft) gaps between the offsets and allow 90 cm (3 ft) between the rows, with the growing tip just below the surface of the soil. If the weather is dry, keep well watered until the plants start to produce strong growth.

If persistent perennial weeds are a problem in your garden and cannot be controlled by the mulching methods described in Chapter 4, a permanent mulch can be laid down to allow the comfrey to flourish without the competition of the weeds.

There are groundcover materials used by the horticultural trade (especially those specializing in greenhouse and polythene tunnel crops) and garden centres to give labour-saving weed control. One such material is Mypex. It is a woven polypropylene fabric developed to suppress weeds yet allow water and air into the soil through the fabric mesh. This material can be used in the comfrey bed.

The fabric should be laid over the empty bed, the edges turned into trenches round the bed then held in place by re-filling the trench with the soil. The position of the plants is marked out on the fabric and an 'X' cut is made with a sharp knife. The cut is opened out and the offsets are planted in the soil. The fabric will control the weeds yet allow the rain, air and liquid feeds through to the roots.

HARVESTING

Comfrey is grown for its leaves and stems, which are the richest known source of potassium (potash). The roots can go down into the soil for over 1.8 m (6 ft), gathering minerals and trace elements which are then stored in the stems and leaves and released when these decompose.

Growth starts in early spring and is ready for the first cut by mid-spring, by which time the plants will have produced about 60 cm (2 ft) of growth. Cuts can be taken at four week intervals to give around five cuts per season, the last cut being taken in the early autumn. The plants will continue to grow after this last cut, but the foliage is allowed to die on the plants to allow the nutrients to go back into the roots to build them up for the next year.

Newly planted offsets should only be cut twice in the first season in early and late summer. All flower heads must be removed during this first year to allow the plant to fully establish itself.

Cut the stems and leaves with a sharp knife or a pair of garden shears about 5 cm (2 in) above the soil. The stems are covered with hairs which can cause skin irritation so you would be wise to wear a pair of gloves.

PLANT CARE

To maintain such a high yield of leaves, the plants require a little care and attention during the growing season. They must be well watered in dry weather and to ensure the soil is rich, regular feeding is recommended. A mulch of compost or well rotted manure after the first cut has been taken can be followed by another mulch mid-summer. Failing that, a dressing of blood, fish and bone should be applied at a rate of 110 gm per sq m

(4 oz per sq yd) and hoed into the top layers of the bed. A liquid feed of its own juice can be given at two-week intervals.

If the bed is covered with Mypex then the mulching cannot be carried out without lifting the covering, and then there is the difficulty of relaying it. A seaweed liquid feed should be used in its place, applied as recommended on the container.

USING COMFREY

In an organic garden comfrey is used as a plant food. The leaves and stems can be used as they are, as a mulch or turned into a liquid feed. This latter is valuable because of the high level of potash it contains – ideal for potash-loving plants.

LEAVES AND STEMS

When using the comfrey in the leaf and stem form it is advisable to allow them to wilt for a day or two to avoid the possibility of some of the stems taking root and starting to grow again.

As a cut can be taken in mid-spring it can be used as a potato fertilizer. The seed potatoes are lain in the bottom of the trench and the wilted comfrey leaves are laid on top of them; the trench is then filled with soil. As the leaves decay they will release their potash-rich fertilizer, boosting the young potato shoots into sturdy plants.

The comfrey leaves are also a valuable addition to the runner bean trench and, as I mentioned in the section on worm compost (see page 43), comfrey leaves can be used as a mulch in the greenhouse to feed the tomatoes.

The leaves and stems can be added to the compost.

They produce little or no fibre as they rot down so are not of any real value in providing bulk. However they are an excellent activator, encouraging bacterial activity to generate heat in the heap.

LIQUID

The average garden does not have a sufficiently large bed of comfrey for it to make any significant difference to the soil as a whole, using it as a leaf and stem mulch. The best way to use comfrey to ensure the greatest value to the whole garden is in a liquid form. Comfrey liquid can be made in two ways, by soaking the leaf and stem in water to give a ready-to-use solution, or by collecting the juice from the decaying leaves which results in a comfrey concentrate which needs to be diluted before use.

This concentrated liquid is diluted with water between 10 and 30 times and is used throughout the garden and on houseplants. It can be applied to the soil to feed the plants via their roots or sprayed on the foliage for the nutrients to be absorbed through the leaves (foliar feeding).

For general use a once-a-week feed of 15:1 dilution will keep the garden healthy. Apply from a watering can using a fine rose or a spray/feeder attachment on the end of a hose. All plants will benefit from a foliar feed – the vegetable patch, herbaceous border, rose- and summer-bedding borders, patio tubs, house plants and even the lawn. Give the plants a good soaking, the excess running off the leaves will not be lost as it will feed the soil.

For potatoes and tomatoes increase the concentration to 10:1, but only use the watering can on the tomatoes as the hose is too fierce and will damage the plants. The tomatoes need feeding twice a week.

Making liquid comfrey

READY-TO-USE SOLUTION

I believe this method has several disadvantages and I cannot really recommend its use. However many gardeners do use it as it is very simple to make. Here is the process anyway!

Method 13.5 kg (30 lb) of leaves and stems are added to 180 l (40 gal) of water and allowed to stand for three to four weeks. At the end of this period the solution is ready for use. It is not diluted further. Some gardeners use the rainwater barrel, collecting water from the shed or greenhouse roof. Every time it rains the solution will be diluted further, making it difficult to know exactly what strength is being used and when to add more comfrey to make another solution.

Now to the disadvantages of this method. As the stems and leaves are in the solution they start to break down into little pieces which get into the watering can and block the holes in the rose. A minor problem compared to the fact that the solution stinks! The leaves breaking down in the water is a putrefaction process and the smell is appalling. Not a process to use if you wish to remain on good terms with your relations and neigh-bours! The smell can be controlled if a sealed container is used but it still clings to hands and clothing and stays in the air for a time after use.

COMFREY CONCENTRATE

This second method is the one I would recommend. There is no smell at all and the product is pleasant to use.

As the leaves and stems decay they readily release a juice which can be collected. This is concentrated comfrey liquid which needs to be diluted before use. All that is needed is a container with a good fitting lid. It is

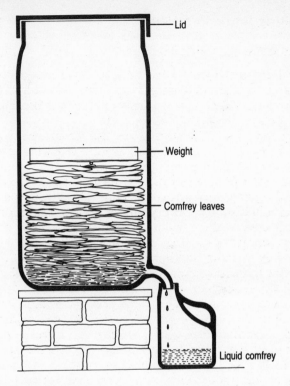

FIG. 7 Making liquid comfrey.

best if it is made of plastic as metal tends to rust. Any size will do, from a bucket to a 180 l (40 gal) water barrel. The larger the container the more comfrey it will hold and the more juice will be extracted. Make a hole 1–2 cm (½–¾ cm) in diameter in the side wall, as near to the bottom as possible, and push a piece of plastic or copper tube into it to channel the juice into a collecting bottle (Fig. 7). The tube must be a tight fit in the hole to prevent leakage. The container should also be raised on bricks so that the collecting bottle can stand beneath it. Empty plastic fruit juice bottles are ideal for collecting the liquid.

The container is filled with comfrey leaves and stems, and a heavy object such as a piece of broken flagstone or a brick, depending on the size of the opening, is laid on top. The weight compresses the comfrey and speeds the release of the juice. The lid is replaced on the container and around three or four weeks later a dark brown sweet-smelling liquid starts to drip from the tube.

As the bulk of the foliage starts to decay the rate the liquid flows will increase, so keep an eye on the bottle as one day it will be only half full and the next it will be overflowing.

Keep topping up the container with fresh comfrey to maintain a continuous supply, so as to build up a stock for use the following year in the period before the new season's comfrey is ready to cut. A 180 l (40 gal) container will produce about 23 l (5 gal) of concentrated liquid.

At the end of the season clean out the comfrey sludge from the container in readiness for next year. The sludge is added to the New Zealand bin.

This concentrated liquid, as I previously mentioned, can be diluted between 10 and 30 times with water. Some gardeners prefer to use the 30:1 rate, adopting the policy of frequent feeding with a weaker feed. In this case the time between feeds will be halved.

To enhance the comfrey liquid further, nettles can be added to the container to produce an exceptionally beneficial plant food. It is possible to use nettles on their own to make a rich foliar feed and this process is detailed in Chapter 11, p. 91.

COMFREY PEAT

As the HDRA are the leading authority on comfrey, it is a regular feature in their newsletter, which often includes reports of work carried out by amaetur gardeners. One such piece of work was the development of a soilless compost called 'comfrey peat'. It consisted of putting alternate laters of comfrey and peat in a container – 10 cm (4 in) of each – covering to keep out the rain, then leaving it while the comfrey rotted down. The peat absorbs the released liquid to produce a rich material for use in own-made potting composts or mulching in the greenhouse. However, as peat is not an ecologically acceptable product, it is recommended that you try alternatives. Leafmould is the best but the peat-substitute coconut fibre 'coir' can also be used to produce a comfrey-rich product.

This comfrey mixture can be made in a polythene sack, a dustbin or, for larger quantities, a New Zealand bin. The size of the container will be determined by the quantity of comfrey leaves and stems available.

CHAPTER 8

GREEN MANURES

Nature will not tolerate bare soil. If any soil is left bare, grasses and weeds will germinate and cover the ground very quickly. At the end of their life cycle the grasses and weeds rot down and their nutrients return to the soil. This is Nature's way of maintaining uncultivated land in a fertile condition.

The gardener can make use of this principle and grow a crop on land which would otherwise have been left vacant for part of a season, with the intention of returning this crop to the soil. This is called a 'green manure'.

You will note that this 'manure' bears no relation to that from animals, although the end purposes are very much the same.

With all the different products available to feed the soil, you may wonder why there is any need to grow a 'green manure' as well. The answer is that it is very difficult to make enough compost to fill all the uses you could put it to and it may not always be possible to supplement the compost with animal manures, so any shortfall can be filled with a green manure. They can offer many advantages to the grower, although I do not believe they are an alternative to compost making and the mulching techniques.

Another advantage of green manures is that many of them attract beneficial insects into the garden, aiding the pollination of flowers and the fight against pests.

ADVANTAGES OF USING A GREEN MANURE

Soil which is left uncovered or uncultivated over a period of time presents two problems. In the summer months it will be covered with weeds which will then seed, creating even more weeds. This will cause a lot of work to keep them under control, and not only will they compete for nutrients with any cultivated plants you may wish to grow, but the weeds can also be host to various pests and diseases.

Over the winter months the bare soil is at the mercy of the elements. Heavy rains will leach the nutrients out of the soil and, if the ground slopes, erosion will occur with the finer particles being washed down to the bottom of the slope.

A green manure will act as a weed suppressor, smothering anything which attempts to compete with the manure. The root structure of the plants will hold the soil structure together preventing erosion taking place. Another advantage is that the roots absorb the nutrients from the soil, which are then stored in the crop, preventing them from being leached by the rains.

The foliage acts as an umbrella breaking the force of the raindrops, again helping to maintain the soil structure. The foliage also protects the soil from frosts, keeping the ground temperatures higher so that the soil organisms continue to be active over the colder months.

Green manures help to increase the fertility of the soil. Some varieties have an extensive root system going deep into the soil, absorbing nutrients which would be out of reach to the shallower-rooted plants. When the green manure is dug into the soil it releases these nutrients for other plants to use.

Many of the plants which are used as green manures are 'nitrogen fixation' plants. This means they have the ability to absorb nitrogen from the air and store it in the plant. It is then released into the soil as the plant decays.

The act of returning the green manure to the soil is also adding organic matter to the soil again helping to provide humus to build up a good soil structure. This can be done either by digging in the crop at the appropriate time or by cutting down the foliage for adding to the compost heap. The recommended treatment for most of the green manures is that they are turned into the soil at the appropriate time in their growing cycle. Earlier I gave a number of reasons why digging is not such a good idea (see page 33) so what do you do if you do not wish to dig?

The choice of green manures will allow you to select crops which can be cut down and left to rot into the soil. Fodder raddish will disappear completely after cutting but other varieties will leave the root structure. If the green manures have been used in the decorative part of the garden this will not create a problem as mulching the soil around the plants with newspaper under the organic material will suppress any tendency for the green manure to grow again. However in the vegetable plot this can be a problem for it will be difficult to sow seed if the soil is full of roots. Green manures therefore need to be considered in relation to the crop rotation plan. It is best to follow the green manure with a crop which means the ground will be disturbed, such as trenching out for potatoes.

Gardening is not a series of individual events; each is a part of a closely interwoven programme and as such every action must be considered in relation to its effect on the whole garden.

SOWING GREEN MANURES

Which green manure you sow will depend on which time of the year the ground is vacant. Most gardeners fill their gardens during the summer months and empty them over the winter. There are occasions when, for instance, the plot needs a rest for it may have become run down by years of neglect, over cropping, or it may be infested with a soil pest or disease. In these cases a summer sowing or even a perennial green manure can be used.

The principle is simple: sow the seed, let the plant grow for as long as possible to produce the maximum of leaf, but do not allow the plant to flower or produce seed. Then when the land is needed, either turn it into the soil or cut the foliage and gather it for composting.

Green manures can be sown at any time except in the depth of winter. Sow early spring for a summer crop, or in the vegetable plot when a quick-maturing variety can be grown to precede a main crop vegetable which will not be sown or planted until early summer. Green manures can be sown through to the late autumn for the overwintering variety to protect the soil from the winter weather.

Naturally the correct variety of seed must be chosen for, like all plants, some are summer- and some winter-growing varieties. The wrong choice of seed will lead to disappointment as either the seed will not germinate or the foliage will be killed by the frosts before it can do its job.

There are some dwarf varieties of green manures which can be sown in areas being cultivated not only to suppress the weeds but also to add nitrogen to the soil. The Brussels sprout plot is a good example where this type of planting can be successful. There is sufficient space between the sprouts to sow a crop of clover. I have also sown agricultural lupins in the cabbage plot, which are not much benefit in suppressing weeds but do add nitrogen and give a good return for the compost heap.

Follow the sowing instructions provided with the

seed. Some are sown broadcast and need to be protected from the birds. (Green manures are too expensive to treat like grass seed, which are sown thickly enough to compensate for that taken by the birds.) The simplest method is to rake the soil before sowing, thereby forming small furrows, spread the seed then rake again at right angles to the first raking to cover the seed.

Other varieties are sown in rows (drills), in the same way carrot or beetroot seed are sown. Space the seed at 5–8 cm (2–3 in) apart with a 15 cm (6 in) gap between rows.

GREEN MANURE SEEDS

AGRICULTURAL CHICORY

This is a very valuable deep-rooted plant which brings minerals up to the surface as well as leaving it in a very friable state. This variety cannot be eaten and it is not to be confused with the edible vegetable. It can be sown with clover or on its own and is beneficial on poor or impoverished soils. Chicory can be sown at any time throughout the growing season at a rate of 30 gm per sq m (1 oz per sq yd).

AGRICULTURAL LUPINS

This is one of the most attractive of the green manures, producing a profusion of deep blue flowers. As a member of the pea family it has the ability to fix nitrogen in the soil. The roots penetrate deep into the subsoil bringing up some of the rarer trace elements and making them available to the surface soil.

Sow at any time during the growing season from early spring to mid-summer. Sow the seeds in drills, 8 cm (3 in) apart 2.5 cm (1 in) deep with 15 cm (6 in) between drills.

Lupins do best in acid soils as they dislike alkaline conditions.

AGRICULTURAL MUSTARD

This is one of the fastest growing of the green manures and is ideal for reclaiming, reinvigorating and cleansing soils. It is used as a control for wireworm. It can be sown between mid-spring and late summer at a rate of 30 cm per sq m (1 oz per sq yd).

Note Mustard is a member of the cabbage family and as such is susceptible to clubroot. Do not use on land where the following crop will be brassicas.

ALFALFA

Sometimes called lucerne, alfalfa is a deep-rooted perennial and as such will grow for several years if sown on land being rested. It will survive the winter from a summer sowing, making it an excellent crop to protect the soil from the leaching action of the winter rains. It also guards against erosion. Alfalfa stores up many nutrients and is rich in calcium, phosphorus, potassium and many trace elements, making it a valuable soil conditioner. It dislikes waterlogged, acidic soil conditions. The seed are broadcast thinly at a rate of 30 gm per 10 sq m (1 oz per 10 sq yd)

Alfalfa can also be used as a salad crop eaten in the same way as cress, or used as a sprouting seed grown on the kitchen windowsill.

BUCKWHEAT

This plant grows rapidly and produces a large amount of foliage which not only provides organic matter for the soil but also suppresses adjacent weeds. It is thought to be one of the best green manures for impoverished soils. The roots extend deep into the soil, collecting minerals normally out of the reach of cultivated plants. It has additional value, for a sowing in early spring will attract many of the beneficial insects into the garden such as bees and butterflies and, even more importantly, hoverflies. The hoverfly larvae are voracious feeders on aphids (green and blackfly) and if the buckwheat is sown in the rosebed or close to a bean row, it will help with the control of these pests.

Sow at a rate of 30 gm per sq m (1 oz per sq yd).

CLOVER

Clover provides a very rich source of nitrogen and, if it is allowed to flower, will attract the bees. It does not grow well in poor, acidic soils. Clover can be sown both in the spring and late summer, this latter sowing being left over the winter period as a groundcover crop.

Sow at a rate of 30 gm per 6 sq m (1 oz per 6 sq yd).

FIELD BEANS

Field beans or winter beans are an agricultural variety of the broad bean family, commonly grown as an animal feed as well as a green manure. A very hardy plant and a nitrogen fixer. It can be sown from early to late autumn to stand over the winter months. Allow it to grow to 45 cms (18 in) before cutting it down, leaving the foliage to rot on the soil.

It is broadcast sown at 15 gm per sq m (½ oz per sq yd).

FODDER RADDISH

The sowing dates for this crop are limited and the seed
should be sown preferably in late summer but no later
than early autumn. The crop is left to grow over the
winter when it will die down and be incorporated into
the soil by early spring. Fodder raddish produces a large
amount of foliage, releasing nutrients into the soil which
have been brought to the surface by the deeply-
penetrating root. Raddish is susceptible to carrot-fly
attack so care is needed when this crop is used in the
vegetable plot.

Sow at a rate of 30 gm per sq m (1 oz per sq yd).

HUNGARIAN RYE

This is a cereal rye and not a grass. It has an extensive
root system making it one of the best green manures for
improving the soil structure. Sown from late summer
until mid-autumn, it will overwinter to produce a great
deal of growth in early spring which is best chopped up
with the spade before digging into the soil.

Broadcast the seed at 30 gm per sq m (1 oz per sq yd).

WINTER TARES

These are often referred to as 'vetches' and are fast-
growing nitrogen-fixing plants. Producing a good bushy
growth this crop will provide good weed control. It can
be sown at any time between early spring and mid-
autumn, the later sowings being left to overwinter. It is
an excellent soil conditioner, improving both the
structure and fertility level.

Tares are sown in drills with 5 cm (2 in) between
seeds and 15 cm (6 in) between rows.

CHAPTER 9

ANIMAL MANURES AND STRAW

To supplement the compost made from their own garden waste most gardeners turn to outside sources of organic material which can be easily imported into their garden. One such source is the animal manures.

Unlike the green manures, the term manure in this section is given to the urine and dung (excreta) of animals kept indoors, together with their bedding, which is normally straw, spoilt hay or wood shavings. The manures can be subdivided into farmyard, stable and poultry. The quality of the product can vary considerably, depending on how the animals are kept and fed. The nutrient levels in manures are relatively low and they are looked upon more as a source of organic matter than as a soil fertilizer.

FARMYARD MANURES

These are not as plentiful nowadays because there has been a drift away from bedding cows and pigs in straw. Instead the animals are kept standing on concrete floors which are washed down, and the slurry is collected in tanks to be spread on the fields as a liquid. There are several problems with this but the worst is the smell, mostly caused by the concentrated food the animals are fed on.

However if an old-fashioned farmer can be found who still beds his animals on straw and feeds them on root crops and hay, it is well worth having him deliver a load, especially if you are working on sandy soils.

Note. Beware of pig manures. Pigs can be deficient in copper and as a result be dosed with copper supplements to compensate for this deficiency. Some of the additive is not absorbed and ends up in the dung, giving a high level of copper in the manure. If collecting pig manure check with the farmer if the animals are receiving copper supplements.

STABLE MANURES

Stable manures are the commonest source of imported material in the garden. With the popularity of riding, there are few of us who do not have a riding stable or someone keeping horses within easy reach of their garden. Most are only too pleased to have the manure carted away, as otherwise they have to pay the local council to do so. Some people do charge for it but normally at a reasonable price.

Horse manure is preferable to the farmyard manure because it is a 'hot' manure. This is due to the fact that it rapidly produces heat when stacked. Horse manure was the basis of the hot beds so popular in the gardens of large houses at the turn of the century. The gardener used them to produce early crops, to enable him to offer such treats as having strawberries available for Easter.

There is one problem with stable manure these days and that is many owners are using wood shavings instead of straw for bedding. I would not recommend using this unless you are able to stack the manure for a minimum of two years. Wood shavings decompose very slowly and, if added to the soil in an undecomposed

71

state, can do a great deal more harm than good. They can deplete the soil of nitrogen and, if used as a mulch, will dry out in the summer and turn the soil surface into a bed of sawdust which the rain has difficulty in penetrating. The rain tends to run off leaving the soil dry underneath.

POULTRY MANURE

Fresh poultry manure has for many years been looked upon as an ideal activator for the compost heap. It is the only manure which could be called a soil food as it is very much richer in nitrogen, phosphate and potash than any of the other manures. However, the fresh manure is too 'hot' to come into contact with the plant roots and would damage them if used.

The manure should not be left out in the open or the nitrogen will be lost to the air and the rain will wash out the other nutrients. Keep it under cover until it has cooled down enough, and apply it to the soil a week or so before any seeds are sown.

The 'Organic' movements in the UK are moving away from using 'broiler' poultry manure. Broiler farming is a very cruel and unhealthy method of raising chickens for the table and for laying, with all sorts of drugs being fed to these creatures to minimize the levels of disease in such overcrowded conditions. The Soil Association, the governing body of the organic commercial growers, has banned the use of these manures on ethical grounds. They believe that if you are trying to live by natural laws, a by-product from such an unnatural source is unacceptable.

The compost from barn-kept poultry is acceptable. Often they are bedded down on peat, making this an even more valuable product.

MANAGING MANURES

All manures need to be stacked until well rotted down to be of most benefit to the soil. The straw in fresh manure needs nitrogen for its decomposition process and if dug into the soil will rob the latter to meet its own needs. It can be used fresh as a mulch and weed suppressor, but there is the problem that it will dry out in the dry weather and can then be blown about in the wind.

To stack manure build a heap about 1.2 m (4 ft) square, and about the same height. Water every 15 cm (6 in) if it is dry. The layers can be trodden down to compress the manure to help build up the heat quickly. Once the heap is built, cover it with black polythene sheeting and leave it for two to three months, by which time it will have broken down into a beautiful material for improving the soil.

Manures can also be added to the New Zealand bin and mixed in along with the vegetable compost, but this is not as good as stacking it on its own. *Do not* add any manure except perhaps poultry when used as an activator to the compost bin.

Use the rotted manure as you would compost, either digging it into the soil or mulching at any time of the year.

STRAW

With the diminishing supply of farmyard manures and the increasing use of wood chips in the stables, many gardeners are turning to straw to supplement their compost requirements.

There are two problems with using straw:

1. There is very little organically grown straw available, and what there is can be expensive. If chemically grown straw is used every effort must be made to ensure all pesticide and other chemical residues have been degraded to an organically acceptable level.
2. Straw does not rot down as easily as vegetable waste or manures so more care has to be taken during its processing.

If you become involved in the science of materials decomposing and their relationship with the soil and the bacterial activity in the soil, one term you are likely to come across is the carbon/nitrogen ratio. In well made compost the ratio is about 10:1. This means in the material there are 10 parts of carbon for every one of nitrogen. The higher the ratio, the more difficult it becomes to break down the material into a plant food/soil conditioner.

Straw has a carbon/nitrogen ratio of about 100:1. Wood chippings have a ratio of 500:1; hence my recommendation to avoid these.

Straw left lying in its baled condition will not break down very rapidly because of the high ratio. If dug into the soil it will eventually break down but it needs to reduce the carbon/nitrogen ratio and in order to do that will rob the soil of nitrogen. However with help it can be converted into a usable material relatively easily.

Try whenever possible to obtain straw from the previous season's crop, as this gives it the opportunity to have lost much of its chemical residues. An alternative is to stack the bales yourself and allow them to weather for a year in an area where if the chemicals are washed out they will not harm crops grown on that area at a later date. On the other hand, the experts do estimate that the vast majority of residues are rendered harmless in new straw if the straw heap is built properly and works correctly.

THE STRAW HEAP

Straw needs to be thoroughly soaked before being stacked and the only effective way to do this is to split the bales and turn the hose on them. It is difficult to say how much water will be needed; this you must decide for yourself as a great deal depends on the previous treatment of the bale. Was it in a barn all winter keeping the frost off the potatoes and carrots? In this case it will be extremely dry and will need a lot of watering. If it was just lying outside, exposed to the weather, it will not require nearly so much.

While watering, pull the bales apart as much as possible for, as with compost making, air is an essential element and the less compacted the straw the more air is trapped into the heap. Like the compost heap the straw heap works best when built on the soil.

Start to build the heap by laying out a 1.2 m by 15 cm (4 ft by 6 in) thick layer of straw. If there are any signs of dryness, give this layer another soaking. Next, two to three handfuls of a high nitrogen activator need to be sprinkled over the straw and watered in to promote the decomposition. Poultry manure is the best for it already contains the bacteria which specialize in breaking down the cellulose in the straw. Dried blood is as good if the poultry manure is unavailable. Also sprinkle 110 gm (4 oz) of ground limestone over the layer to neutralize the acids formed during the decomposition process.

Continue to build the heap in 15 cm (6 in) layers, adding the activator and limestone each time and watering again if necessary.

As oxygen plays an important role during the early stages of the process, do not squeeze the entrapped air out of the heap by treading it down. It will settle under its own weight, still maintaining sufficient air in the layers.

The heap must be built quickly, preferably within a

few hours, and no longer than over a day to retain the moisture in the straw and to encourage the rapid build-up of heat for the first stage of decomposition.

When the heap is built, cover it with a sheet of black polythene sheeting, holding down the edges firmly to prevent it from blowing off in the wind. As the heap settles and shrinks keep the polythene cover tight by pulling it down and refastening it.

Unlike compost there is no need to turn over the straw after a few weeks, however do make sure it does not dry out. Any signs of it becoming dry, water it again.

In about three months the centre of the heap will be a nice friable material ready to use on the soil. The outside edges may still not have rotted down completely and this can be incorporated in your next straw heap.

As with the other alternatives to compost, straw does not have the same high nutrient level or soil conditioning ability and is therefore not a replacement. It is, however, a great benefit to the areas which would otherwise be left untreated.

CHAPTER 10

ORGANIC FERTILIZERS AND SOIL CONDITIONERS

Organic products, whether they are fertilizers or soil conditioners, are slow acting. This is because they rely upon the soil life to break them down into the condition needed by the plants to absorb them, in the case of fertilizers, or to improve the quality of the soil, in the case of a soil conditioner.

This is why organic gardeners must think ahead maybe even several months, when considering the condition of the soil and the food needs of plants to be grown in it. You need to remember that even applying an organic fertilizer tomorrow, it will take several weeks before its nutrients become available to the plant. The plant will be growing and may begin to show deficiency symptoms in the interim period.

In organic gardening very little happens overnight. If converting to organic growing on heavily chemical-contaminated soils or impoverished soils, do not expect immediate results, but as each year goes by improvements will be seen and there will be rewards for the patience required to work with Nature.

Although the term 'fertilizer' and 'soil improver' are often mentioned in one breath, there is a difference between the two.

FERTILIZERS

A fertilizer is a plant food and is often referred to as minerals or elements. It could be a combination of different minerals or elements depending on the specific needs of the plants. Although this in some ways goes against the organic principle of only feeding the soil, there are occasions when individual plants require special treatment and the single or multiple-element fertilizers provide it.

Fertilizers are normally in a granular form, easy to spread by the handful, but some can be turned into a liquid form.

SOIL CONDITIONERS

Soil conditioners are really concentrated organic matter. Although they contain plant foods their major role is to improve the soil by activating the soil micro-organisms to work both on the organic fertilizer and the compost etc., which have been added to the soil to create a highly fertile growing medium – your garden.

Soil conditioners are used in conjunction with organic matter and not as a substitute for compost, leafmould, manure etc., which in themselves are all soil conditioners.

IS IT ORGANIC?

Organic fertilizers and soil conditioners are normally purchased products. Garden centres stock some of the popular items but for whole-range availability, it will be necessary to contact the organic-growing specialists (see pages 93, 94).

For the newcomer to organic cultivation, contacting the latter is probably the best advice for it is not always obvious whether or not you have the right product.

For an example, many bags quote the words 'organic', yet the product is not acceptable to the organic gardener. There are available a wide range of 'organically based' fertilizers. As mentioned earlier, all organic products are slow acting and these organic-based fertilizers contain fast-acting chemical fertilizers to overcome the time problem associated with the slower release of the organic nutrients. For this reason they are chemical fertilizers and not organic.

There are also some wholly organic fertilizers which are not acceptable for they contain a highly soluble natural product such as Chilean Potassium Nitrate which has been banned by the organic growers' governing bodies.

The same applies to the soil conditioners. Many of these are based on poultry manures and I have already discussed the broiler business. Many have also been found to contain large quantities of heavy metals and other chemicals which makes them unsuitable for use by the organic gardener.

How do you know which to choose? The simplest answer is to use a product bearing the Soil Association symbol. Alternatively, contact the HDRA to find out if they have analyzed the product and approved it.

It is not easy to distinguish which products are suitable for there are quite a number not bearing the Soil Association symbol, or been approved, but nevertheless are truly organic and their use is a great benefit to the garden. Unfortunately with these it boils down to experience. Organic gardeners become 'tuned into' the soil and become aware of what is good for the soil and what is not.

One difficulty an author of a book such as this has is in recommending proprietary products, especially giving trade names and specific suppliers. It is a fact of life that products and manufacturers come and go. As a consequence I have only named those which have been available over a considerable period in the past and I believe will be so for some time to come.

My advice is that you become aware of new products as they become available.

ORGANIC FERTILIZERS

Although many believe the addition of organic matter only in the form of compost, manures, leaf mould etc., is all that is needed to keep the soil healthy, I believe that as the nutrient level of these is relatively low, there is a need to boost food levels by the addition of fertilizers. This is especially true in the case of specialist varieties and more importantly in the vegetable plot which will face intensive cultivation.

The contents list on a fertilizer bag can be very confusing to a beginner, for in the majority of cases the active ingredients are listed by the chemical symbol of the element. Nitrogen is identified by N, phosphorous as P, potassium as K, calcium as Ca, and so on. Quite often you will see the term 'NPK fertilizer' but more so in the chemical-growing literature.

Unfortunately it can be even more confusing, for the amount of each element available to the plants is quoted in the oxide forms: for instance the amount of phosphorous would be seen as 5% P_2O_5. It is not important to fully understand what it all means but if you are deciding between different products, it is helpful to be able to compare like with like.

The recommended rate for applying a fertilizer is listed in gm per sq m (oz per sq yd). It is not always possible to measure out the quantities so an easy-to-remember rule of thumb is:

1 handful = 55 gm (2 oz)

Some fertilizers are heavier or lighter than others, so the weight of a handful will vary, but not by too much.

Remember an over-application of an organic fertilizer will not harm the plants or the soil, but do not overdo it as you cannot speed up the process by adding more than is required.

As organic fertilizers are the product of Nature's manufacturing, there can be variations from source to source and even within a single source, so the exact levels of the nutrients cannot always be guaranteed. An analysis quoted on the bag is therefore an average figure for the product. It is quite common to find variations for the same product produced by different manufacturers.

The elements for good growth are further divided into the 'major elements', so called as they are present and required by the plants in relatively large amounts, and the 'trace elements' which are only available and required in much smaller quantities. The major elements present will be measured as a % of the total, whereas the trace elements are in such small quantities they will be quoted as being present in 'parts per million' (ppm).

Both major and trace elements are essential components for our health so it is important they are in the plants we eat, and they can only get them from the soil.

Let us look at the various organic sources of these elements. Remember, however, that it is always better to use the more balanced products for building up a healthy soil.

SEAWEED – THE BALANCED FERTILIZER

Seaweed is one of the most important sources of both major and trace elements. It grows in the richest garden known to man – the sea. Its real value lies in its richness in trace elements, including many which are not available in any other source.

Coming from a living plant seaweed fertilizer is well balanced, containing neither too much nor too little of any one element. Being well balanced it is safe to use from the point that an over application will not result in any imbalance of elements in the soil.

Seaweed also encourages baterial activity within the soil, releasing locked up minerals and helping the development of good root systems, as well as supplying its own range of nutrients to build a high level of soil fertility.

However, due to the pollution of our seas many people are becoming concerned about its use. In its fresh state, seaweed could be a problem, depending on the effluent being pumped into the surrounding seas. Near a nuclear power plant there is always the chance of radioactive contamination. Another contaminant is oil and any affected seaweed must be avoided.

All the processed forms are very safe to use.

Fresh Seaweed   Seaweed taken direct from the beach can be used either as a mulch or composted. If applied as a mulch it is at its best in spring and early summer for at that time of year it is much richer in nutrients. If spread on the soil and left uncovered it will dry out and go brittle, start to smell and attract flies. It is best covered with grass cuttings, compost or straw to prevent this happening.

As there will still be traces of salt on the seaweed, it needs to be hosed down to remove this before being spread on the soil, or the salt could have a detrimental effect on the plants. This is not so important if the seaweed is being used to mulch the vegetable plot in the autumn because the salt will have been neutralized by the time the growing season comes round again in the spring.

The best way to treat fresh seaweed is to compost it. Let the seaweed dry for two or three days to lose a large proportion of its water content. As with all excessive water release in the compost process putrefaction occurs, resulting in an unpleasant smell.

The seaweed can be added to a New Zealand bin, layering the compost and seaweed in alternate 15 cm (6 in) layers. It is then left until the seaweed has decomposed to a state similar to compost.

Being a rich source of potash this seaweed compost is an ideal mulch material for tomatoes, both greenhouse and outdoor varieties.

Fresh seaweed does have one disadvantage unless your garden backs straight onto the beach – transportation. It is very bulky and wet. Polythene bags, tied tightly at the neck are needed and preferably carried in a trailer, not the car.

Its virtues are that it provides a weed-, pest- and disease-free compost, even if a great deal is needed because it rots down to almost nothing.

Processed Seaweed Products   Seaweed is available in a more convenient form for transporting and applying to the soil and can be purchased as a powder or a liquid from a garden centre or horticultural supplies merchant. The seaweeds applied in these forms are very versatile, making them indispensable in the garden.

Seaweed Meal   Seaweed meal is produced from the 'bladder' type of seaweed and is harvested from seaweed beds off the coastline of several northern hemisphere countries. Its collection is strictly controlled and methods must be used to ensure the growth parts of the seaweed are left undamaged to allow them to continue to produce fresh growth for subsequent harvesting.

As with all environmentally friendly processes, the seaweed will still be available for our future generations to use. The seaweed is dried and ground to produce a powder.

The nutritional value of the meal is high both for the soil and for animals and it is used as an animal feed supplement, especially for horses. It is rich in all the major and trace elements as well as containing vitamins, protein, amino acids and carbohydrates.

It is a well balanced product but is slow acting and I believe is best applied in autumn. If adopting the no-dig technique, dress the soil with 240 gm per sq m (8 oz per sq yd), before the newspaper or cardboard weed suppressor is laid down. This then gives it about six months to release its nutrients.

Seaweed meal is very beneficial for the soil, not only as a feed, but also because it encourages bacterial activity. As a result it is often classified as a soil conditioner.

Calcified Seaweed This seaweed product is a coral-like material quarried off the seabed on the Brittany and Cornish coasts. It is in fact dead seaweed which started life on the coasts of the Americas and floated across the Atlantic to the English Channel on the Gulf Stream. The seaweed is lifted off the seabed, dried and crushed for garden use.

Its value over seaweed meal is that it is very rich in calcium (50%) and magnesium (5%), but it has the one disadvantage in that it does not contain any nitrogen. Even so, coupled with the nutritional properties of seaweed, this is a good general fertilizer to use all over the garden, especially where acid conditions need to be made more alkaline.

Calcified seaweed is available from a very fine powder to an extremely coarse one. In fact in the coarse form do not be surprised to find pieces of seashell, which in themselves are a good source of calcium. Although much quicker acting in releasing its nutrients than seaweed meal, the speed of release will also depend upon the particle size of the powder. The very fine is ideal for a dressing in the early spring, being effective by the time the plants need a growing boost. The coarser particle naturally is a little slower, but even so the release time of this product is measured in weeks as against months in the case of the seaweed meal.

For a general application, dress the soil at a rate of 240 gm per sq m (8 oz per sq yd) and if adding to home-made potting compost mix in 225 gm per gl (8 oz per 2 gal) bucketful.

Calcified seaweed is also very much less expensive than seaweed meal so it can be used more extensively (except on acid-loving plants) as a garden fertilizer, keeping the dearer meal for more specific requirements.

Seaweed Liquid Feeds   Seaweed is also available in liquid and powder form for turning into a liquid feed. The advantage of this is that the nutrients can be made more easily available to the plant by not only watering the soil with the liquid but also the leaves.

In liquid form the product Maxicrop Natural Seaweed Extract is a reliable one to use. It is available from garden centres but be careful for Maxicrop also produce the same product in what they call a 'Triple Strength Extract' with chemical additives. Make sure you buy the 'Natural' version.

A seaweed extract with the Soil Association symbol of approval is SM3. The uses are the same as Maxicrop but it can only be obtained from Organic Gardening Sundries suppliers.

THE ESSENTIAL ELEMENTS FERTILIZERS

So far I have discussed only products which add a variety of food elements to the soil to maintain a balanced diet for the plants. However situations arise when it may be felt necessary to use an individual element or a combination of elements to deal with specific circumstances. I do not believe these products should be used for general application but only in cases where a quick boost is needed which cannot be obtained from organic matter or the seaweed.

As these are still relatively slow-acting products, releasing the elements over a period of time, there is no real danger with their use in the short term. If used over long periods then, as with chemical fertilizers, an excess of a single element can lead to toxicity problems.

First let us have a brief look at the role of each element and its effect upon the growth of the plant.

Nitrogen (N)   One of the most important elements of plant life, nitrogen is essential for the growth process in plants. As it is the major constituent of chlorophyll, it is necessary for the production of leaves, giving them their richness in colour. A shortage is shown by stunted growth patterns and unhealthy looking leaves, often pale green to yellow in colour.

Phosphorous (P)   This is the element which develops the root system but is also essential in the maturing of plants, bringing about the ripening of fruits and seeds. A shortage will mean a poorly developed root system unable to absorb the food the plant needs from the soil, resulting in a weak plant with discoloured leaves. The signs are often confused with a nitrogen deficiency.

Potassium (K)   Often referred to as potash, potassium is essential for the growth process and is of particular importance in the development of fruit. A shortage shows up as a thinning of the stems of the plants; leaves develop scorch marks around their edges or begin to lose their colour and eventually die off. Potatoes turn black when boiled. A shortage can be the result of excessive use of high nitrogen of phosphate fertilizer.

Calcium (Ca) This is required for the growing function of a plant and to promote good root development. It is also important in correcting the acidity levels of the soil back to a neutral state (pH control). Symptoms of a shortage are shown by stunted growth. Roots fail to develop, the growing tip and shoots become ragged and the plant is prone to disease.

Magnesium (Mg) Essential for the formation of chlorophyll and works with phosphorous in the ripening of seeds. A shortage of magnesium is indicated by stunted growth and the loss of colour in the leaves, showing first in the older leaves, then spreading to the young leaves.

FERTILIZERS

Bonemeal Probably the richest source of phosphorous, with between 20 and 30% phosphate. It is very slow acting and needs to be applied in the autumn to be of any value for the spring sowings. A general application is at a rate of 240 gm per sq m (8 oz per sq yd).

The outbreak of BSE, or 'mad cow disease' as it is popularly known, has raised concern over the use of animal blood and bone products in the garden. There is a belief that with the ban on the use of these in animal food products, the excess will be channelled into the horticultural industry. There is as yet no evidence that BSE can affect people. Even so the HDRA have raised this concern with the supplier of their animal-based fertilizers and have asked for confirmation that the temperatures reached during the sterilization process in the manufacture of these products is sufficient to kill off the disease.

The HDRA are satisfied with the assurances given and believe under the present circumstances their products are safe to use. However they are to continue to monitor the situation and if any new evidence arises which indicates these animal fertilizers could spread BSE, the products will be withdrawn from sale.

Blood, Fish and Bonemeal This is a popular combination fertilizer containing 2–5% nitrogen, 5–8% phosphate and 1–6% potassium. The quick release of nitrogen encourages plant growth, allowing this product to be applied in the early spring. The phosphate and potassium content is released slowly over the growing period to develop the root system and maintain the general health of the plant. Apply at a rate of 120 gm per sq m (4 oz per sq yd).

Dried Blood A very fast acting, high nitrogen (12%) fertilizer. Because of its quick rate of nitrogen release, it is best applied early to mid-summer at a rate of 30 gm per sq m (1 oz per sq yd).

Referring back to the point that one of the reasons chemical fertilizers are bad for the soil is the quick release of the nutrients (see page 11), unfortunately one or two of the organic products fall into this category as well, and blood is one of these. As a result the Soil Association have withdrawn it from their list of approved products for if it is used continuously to boost commercial crops then it is detrimental to the soil.

However, I believe that dried blood can still be used for adding nitrogen to straw, to aid the decomposition process, for it will not then be applied to the soil in the readily soluble form.

Hoof and Horn Meal Another high nitrogen fertilizer (13%) but much slower acting than blood. Apply as a general nitrogen fertilizer at a rate of 120 gm per sq m (4 oz per sq yd). It is also a valuable additive to the home-made potting composts at a rate of 30 gm per 9 l (1 oz per 2 gal) bucketful.

Rock Phosphate   This is a very slow-acting fertilizer, the phosphate content (13%) being released over a number of years. A single dressing will last until the crop rotation cycle (three to four years) brings in the need for another application.

Apply at a rate of 240 gm per sq m (8 oz per sq yd) at any time of the year.

Rock Potash   A high potash (potassium) fertilizer (10%) releasing its nutrient slowly over a two- to three-year period. Again one application in the crop rotation cycle suffices. It can be applied at any time of the year at a rate of 240 gm per sq m (8 oz per sq yd)

All fertilizers are expensive and to reduce the outlay at any one time many of them are available in small packets 1 kg (2.2 lb) However, this is a very expensive way to purchase fertilizers. You pay very much more buying it this way than you would if you bought it in a large 25 kg (55 lb) bag. The savings made can go towards some other item needed for the garden.

Fertilizers keep well if they are not allowed to become damp. A large bag can be used over a season or two, or perhaps if a large bag is too much for your own requirements you can still save money by splitting it with other gardeners.

Mail order can be expensive if carriage is an added extra, so approach the garden centre first and ask them to order the large-sized bag if it is not in stock.

SOIL CONDITIONERS

There are a number of proprietary soil conditioners available which can be used to supplement your own compost. They are not a substitute for your own-made materials for they are applied to the soil in handfuls and not by the barrowload as is the case with compost, leafmould and manure.

You may not see noticeable improvements in the soil within the first year but with time you will see a reward for your efforts.

The following are some of the soil conditioners which bear the approval of the Soil Association.

GOLDEN GROW

Based on poultry manure Golden Grow is rich in nitrogen, phosphorous, potassium and the trace elements. The poultry manure is well composted, reaching the temperatures needed to sterilize it and ensure it is weed free.

SUPER NATURAL ORGANIC COMPOST

This is based on cow manure, peat and bark, and is not very rich in the major food elements. It is used more as a supply of organic matter to the soil.

COMPOSTED BARK

One soil conditioner which is now becoming popular is composted bark. Originally a waste product from the timber industry, enlightened councils are now shredding all the tree prunings and using them in their horticultural programmes. Bark is probably more commonly used on paths and herbaceous beds to suppress the weeds and retain the moisture, but in the composted form it is a benefit to the soil, helping to break up heavy clay soils, and in light sandy soils retaining the much needed moisture.

Bark is low in food nutrients so can only be considered as a soil conditioner.

CHAPTER 11

HOME-MADE FOLIAR FEEDS

The use of comfrey has previously been discussed as a foliar feed (see Chapter 7). There are, however, other plants and products which will make a rich liquid to feed the soil and the plants.

LIQUID NETTLES

One of the commonest plants around us today, and also one of the richest in its mineral content, is the nettle. The root system is capable of collecting many nutrients unavailable to the shallow-rooted plants, making this a valuable plant for feeding both in terms of the garden and for us.

The leaves are the important part for making a liquid feed but it is not worth the bother stripping them off the stems, so the whole stem is used. Nettles do not part with their nutrients as easily as comfrey and the best method is to soak them in a barrel of water. This can be done in the rainwater barrel but again, as with the comfrey, you have no control over the strength of the resulting liquid.

If you can use a barrel specifically for this purpose, fill it with nettles but do not compress them. Add 4.5 l (1 gal) of water for every 0.5 kg (1 lb) of nettles, cover the top with a lid to keep out the rain and leave for three to four weeks. By this time there will be a well balanced liquid feed in the barrel.

Dilute this liquid in the ratio of 1 part to 10 of water and use throughout the garden and on houseplants.

If the solution is to be sprayed through a fine rose or syringe, it is best to strain it through a fine meshed material first to take out any of the nettle residue. An old pair of tights is ideal for the job. It is particularly important to do this if seed heads were used, as these must not be spread around the garden.

LIQUID MANURE

This is made by soaking a bag of manure in a barrel of water. Any well rotted manure can be used – cow, horse or poultry. Put two 9 l (2 gal) bucketfuls of the manure in a coarse hessian sack (polythene is no use as the sack needs to be porous) and immerse in 90 l (20 gal) of water. After six to seven days the resultant liquid will be ready for use, undiluted. Although this liquid is not as rich as the nettle or comfrey, it is a useful feed throughout the garden.

You should never apply liquid feed to dry soil. Water the soil thoroughly first or wait until it has rained. If using liquid feed as a foliar feed, do not spray the plants in the full heat of the sun because the leaves will be scorched. Spray when the sun has moved away, or in the early morning. It is not good to spray the plants with cold water in the evening as it can chill them.

USEFUL ADDRESSES

ORGANIC GROWERS ASSOCIATIONS

The aim of these associations is to promote and lay down standards for organic horticultural and agricultural growers.

Henry Doubleday Research Association Ltd., (HDRA) Ryton Gardens, Ryton-on-Dunsmore, Coventry CV8 3LG This is the association for the amateur gardener. Membership gives a quarterly newsletter and free entry to their organic gardening demonstrations at Ryton Gardens. Membership is highly recommended.

Soil Association Ltd, 86 Colston Street, Bristol BS1 5BB This association determines the standards for food production and as such is of more value to the commercial grower.

SUPPLIERS

Organic product supplier	HDRA or Chase Organics (GB) Ltd, Addlestone, Weybridge, Surrey KT15 1HY.
Garottabin	Sinclair Horticultural & Leisure plc., Firth Road, Lincoln LN6 7AN.
Turning Worms (potting compost made by worms)	The Worm Firm Ltd PO Box 3, Whitland, Dyfed SA34 0BZ or HDRA
Black polythene	Weldbank Plastic Co. Ltd, Devonshire Road, Chorley, PR7 2BY

Organibox   The Halifax Wireform Co. Ltd,
                       Calder Mill, Hebdon Bridge,
                       West Yorkshire.

Mypex   Amoco Fabrics (UK) Ltd,
                       1 Tabley Court, Victoria Street,
                       Altrincham, Cheshire WA14 1EZ

Maxicrop   Stimgro Ltd,
                       Bridge House, 97/101 High Street,
                       Tunbridge, Kent TN9 1DR

Golden Grow   Goldengrow Ltd,
                       Court Farm, Llanover,
                       Abergavenny, Gwent NP7 9XD

Super Natural   Super Natural Ltd,
Organic   Bourne Place Farm,
Compost   Chiddingstone,
                       Edenbridge, Kent TN8 7AR

Composted   Melcourt Industries Ltd,
Bark   Three Cups House,
                       Tetbury GL8 8JG

Coir   East Anglia Products Ltd,
                       11 Langton Place,
                       Bury St. Edmunds IP33 1NE
                       or HDRA

INDEX